# YOU CAN BE A BALLET DANCER

For your first steps into the graceful art
of ballet dancing, Barbara Newman takes
you through a complete ballet class –
from basic rules and postures through
steps and simple sequences to your
closing bows . . .

Also in the YOU CAN series:

YOU CAN BE A GYMNAST
YOU CAN SWIM
YOU CAN RIDE
YOU CAN PLAY CRICKET
YOU CAN PLAY FOOTBALL
YOU CAN PLAY TENNIS

All published by CAROUSEL BOOKS

# YOU CAN BE A BALLET DANCER

A CAROUSEL BOOK 0 552 542385

First published in Great Britain by Carousel Books

PRINTING HISTORY
Carousel edition published 1983

Carousel Books are published by
Transworld Publishers Ltd.,
Century House, 61–63 Uxbridge Road,
Ealing, London W5 5SA

Made and printed by The Guernsey Press Co. Ltd.,
Channel Islands.

# You Can Be A Ballet Dancer

## with Barbara Newman

### Illustrated by Mike Miller

CAROUSEL BOOKS
A DIVISION OF TRANSWORLD PUBLISHERS LTD.

# CONTENTS

A WORD FROM BARBARA NEWMAN . . .    6

EARLY HISTORY OF BALLET    8

MODERN DEVELOPMENTS    13

GETTING STARTED    20
  BASIC REQUIREMENTS FOR THE DANCER    20
    Posture    20
    Turn-out    23
    Line    26

SURROUNDINGS AND EQUIPMENT    29
    Clothing    31
    Floor surface    32
    Music    33
    The barre    34

BASIC POSITIONS OF THE FEET AND ARMS    35
    Feet    35
    Arms    39
    Your body    41

AT THE BARRE    45
  WARMING UP    45
    Warm-up positions    48
    Demi-plié    48
    Grand plié    49
    Relevé    50
    Port de bras    52
  STRETCHING YOUR FEET AND LEGS    56
    Battement tendu    56
  BRUSHING MOVEMENTS: PREPARING TO JUMP    59
    Battement dégagé    59
    Échappé    62
  CIRCULAR MOVEMENTS    64
    Rond de jambe    64
  PREPARING TO BEAT    71
    Frappé    71
    Sur le cou de pied    72

Petit battement 75
ADAGIO 78
Passé 78
Développé 80
Port de bras 83
Fondu 85
Retiré 87
GRANDS BATTEMENTS 91
Balançoire 92

IN THE CENTRE 94
PLACEMENT AND BALANCE 96
ADAGIO 101
Arabesque 101
Attitude 102
JUMPS 111
Sauté, changement and soubresaut 111
Échappé sauté 114
Assemblé 118
Jeté 120
TRAVELLING OR LINKING STEPS 123
Pas de bourrée couru 123
Chassé 125
Glissade 127
TURNS 132
Soutenu 134
Chaîné 137
BIG JUMPS 141
Tour en l'air 141
Changements en tournant 143
Grand jeté 144

CLOSING MOVEMENTS 148

BOWS 150

FAMOUS DANCERS 152

USEFUL ADDRESSES 160
Monthly publications 160

# A WORD FROM BARBARA NEWMAN

The first time I ever went to the ballet, there was a terrible blizzard raging outside the theatre. The wind was howling like a wolf and such thick snow blew along the street that you could hardly see. But inside the theatre, it was warm and still. The world I knew had completely disappeared, and in its place was a kingdom of strange and wonderful creatures. First I saw a flock of swans, flurrying like snow around their majestic queen. Then I visited the Land of Sweets, and watched candy canes and marzipan shepherds whirling at the command of a dainty spun-sugar fairy. And finally I peeked inside the silken tent of a sultan, where golden slaves and veiled harem girls leaped and spun in the flickering light of lanterns.

I was a small child then, smaller than you are now, but I remember my first glimpse of the world of ballet perfectly. The dancers on the stage seemed so magically transformed by the music and their graceful movements that for a long time I couldn't believe they were real people just like me.

Not long afterward, I walked into a ballet studio for the first time. I remember that very clearly too. I climbed a long flight of stairs, opened a white door, and found a tiny dressing room, a shiny black piano, and a large empty studio with sparkling mirrors completely covering one wall. A wooden railing, which I quickly learned was called a barre, ran all the way around the other walls. And so much sunshine poured into the room that the smooth, wooden floor looked like a lake of honey. The moment I put my hand on the barre and opened my feet in first position, my own transformation began. I started to become one of those graceful visions I had seen on the stage that cold, mysterious night.

Most children begin to study ballet when they're about

eight years old. And everyone starts the same way, with one hand on the barre and their feet placed in a certain position by their teacher. That's how I began learning to be a ballet dancer, and that's how you'll begin to learn too. If you're serious about your dancing and want to try more difficult steps, as you get older you might have several lessons in one week. Professional dancers have a lesson every single day, because they know there is always more to learn about this beautiful and difficult art.

Many years passed and I spent thousands of hours in the classroom. But then I injured my ankle so severely that it could not support me properly when I danced, so I never did become a ballet dancer after all. But I've taught dancing and written about it, and talked to many of today's greatest dancers about their own teachers and their training. My teachers over the years have been great dancers too, stars of the world's most famous ballet companies. And I'm still studying and practising. The steps I do in class today are exactly the same steps I first tried to do in that sunny studio so long ago.

Nobody becomes a ballet dancer all by himself. Dancers need teachers — to watch them and guide them and correct their mistakes. That's why you can't learn to dance by reading a book, any more than you can become a ballet dancer by wishing or dreaming.

Think of this book as your introduction to dancing and your welcome from me. I hope it will make you feel at home in the strange world of ballet. I've tried to give you some basic rules, some good advice, and some simple steps to start you on your way. And I'll tell you a secret too. Ballet is great fun. I've always loved doing it, and I've discovered that the harder I work to make every movement perfect, the more fun I have. Even if you never become a dancer, you'll have a wonderful time learning to dance. And if you do want to be a ballet dancer, I hope my book will help you begin.

**Good luck!**

# EARLY HISTORY OF BALLET

The fine art of ballet began during the fifteenth century, at the huge parties of the Italian emperors and noblemen. As celebrations or entertainments for their banquet guests, the royal hosts organised enormous performances that combined dancing, acting, singing and poetry recitation. Catherine of Medici enjoyed these entertainments so much that she brought dancers and singers with her to the French court when she married Henry II and became Queen of France. The same combination of words, action, dance and music appeared in England early in the sixteenth century. King Henry VIII introduced them to his court in a form called the **masque**.

In 1581, a lavish spectacle called *The Comic Ballet of the Queen* (originally, *Le Ballet Comique de la Reine*) was presented at the French court by command of Queen Catherine. Today this work is considered the very first ballet because it united the elements of movement, music and drama for the first time. Until then, they had simply been offered one after the other, without any connection between them.

When Louis XIV became King of France in 1643, ballet was very popular at court, but it was still only performed by the male and female courtiers. There were no professional dancers as there are today. King Louis loved to dance, and he always took the central role in the spectacle for himself, appearing as a god or hero. But he felt that ballet dancing could develop even further and more beautifully if selected people were carefully trained in its movements. So, in 1661 he established the first ballet school in history. It was called the Royal Academy of Dance (*L'Académie Royale de la Danse*).

As this school began producing trained dancers who could execute a refined vocabulary of steps and movements, ballet became professional and its performance left the court and became public. At first only men appeared on the stage, disguising themselves in wigs and masks when they took the women's parts. Women were included in public performances after 1681, but all dancers continued to wear masks on stage for another hundred years. A great male dancer, **Maximilien Gardel**, removed his at one performance in 1722 to let the audience know he was dancing in place of his rival, and masks were abandoned completely in 1773.

Ballet had made great strides by the time dancers were permitted to show their faces on stage. **Jean-Georges Noverre**, a celebrated teacher who was called 'the Shakespeare of the dance', revised the vocabulary of dance steps and created the *ballet d'action* or ballet of action. In this dance form, movement and mime gestures told the entire story of a ballet for the first time, without the help of any spoken words.

Costumes were changing too.

Thin light tunics which revealed the body replaced the men's coats and knee-breeches and the women's heavy, ankle-length skirts. Under these tunics, the dancers wore skin-coloured tights called *maillots*, which were named after the man who made them for the singers and dancers at the Paris Opéra.

Without their restricting costumes, dancers could move more quickly than before, jump higher, and perform many new and different steps. The greatest dancers at that time were **Gaetano Vestris**, widely known as 'the God of the Dance', and his son **Auguste**. Both of them possessed enormous charm and elegance as well as brilliant technique.

In 1820, an Italian ballet master, **Carlo Blasis**, published the first textbook ever written for ballet dancers and their teachers. The plan of instruction he set out in that book organised steps into classroom sequences called *enchaînements*. His clear, logical suggestions have been faithfully passed on, and ballet classes today are still taught according to his methods.

New, lighter subjects for ballet emerged with the new steps and lighter costumes. Greek gods and mythical heroes had been the central characters ever since the lavish productions in which Louis XIV had danced. But when the **Romantic period** began, about 1830, spirits, fairies, ghosts and all sorts of fantastic creatures filled the ballet stages instead. Women wore long, gauzy **tutus** with billowing skirts to dance these characters. **Pointe shoes**, stiffened at the tips so the dancer could turn and balance on the very tips of her toes, added to the ghostly illusion.

After years of importance, men danced more in the background during this period. The greatest Romantic ballets — *La Sylphide* (1832) and *Giselle* (1841) — gave women the starring roles for the first time. Three ballerinas — **Marie Taglioni**, who was the first Sylphide; **Carlotta Grisi**, who was the original Giselle, and **Fanny Elssler** — best captured the Romantic style with the delicacy and grace of their dancing.

Romantic ballet had another side too. In it, for the first time, robust **folk dances** of different countries became part of ballet choreography, appearing alongside the more formal steps. The choreographer of a ballet chooses and arranges its steps just as a composer chooses and arranges musical notes when he writes music. Denmark's greatest choreographer, **August Bournonville**, wrote ballets during the Romantic era that are still danced today exactly as he wrote them over one hundred years ago. One of them is actually called *A Folk Tale*, and his *Napoli* and *Far from Denmark* are also full of comic characters and sunny folk dancing.

The delightful comic ballet *Coppélia* opened in Paris in 1870, just as the Romantic era was ending and important ballet activity was moving to Russia. One man did more than anyone else to carry it there. **Marius Petipa** studied ballet and performed in France before he went to Russia to dance in 1847. He remained in St. Petersburg (now Leningrad) for the rest of his long life, serving in turn as a dancer teacher and choreographer at the Maryinsky Theatre.

Petipa choreographed more than sixty ballets, and filled them with such beautiful and imaginative *enchaînements* that he is now known as 'the father of classic ballet'. Many of his full-evening ballets are still performed. You've probably seen his three greatest creations — *Swan Lake*, *The Sleeping Beauty* and *The Nutcracker* — all of which are danced to Tchaikovsky's sweeping music. Petipa was an old man when he wrote these masterpieces, over seventy years old when *Swan Lake* was completed in 1895, but his choreographic genius is still respected and admired and his works are treasured around the world.

# MODERN DEVELOPMENTS

At the start of this century, the heart of ballet's history lay in Russia. Tsar Nicholas II attended many performances at the Maryinsky Theatre, where Petipa's ballets, the colourful sets and costumes of **Alexandre Benois** and **Leon Bakst** and dozens of brilliant dancers graced the huge stage.

Then, in 1909, a producer named **Serge Diaghilev** brought a troupe of Russian dancers to Paris, where they had such a great success that popular interest in ballet soared again. Diaghilev's Ballets Russes performed in all the major cities in Europe, travelling often to London, Paris and Monte Carlo, and visiting Rome, Vienna, Geneva, Berlin and even North and South America. Stars like **Tamara Karsavina**, **Anna Pavlova** and **Vaslav Nijinsky** appeared in the older ballets they had already performed in Russia — like *Giselle*, *The Sleeping Beauty* and *Swan Lake* — and in new ones which were made for the company every year by young choreographers with new ideas.

Fairies and princes didn't interest **Michel Fokine**, **Leonide Massine**, the dancer Nijinsky, or his talented sister, **Bronislava Nijinska**. They took more realistic subjects for their choreography: acrobats, tennis players, sailers, Spanish peasants, and dancers too became characters in their works. Coaxing the standard ballet steps into new shapes and combinations, they also transformed dancers into an assortment of animals and birds which included a nightingale, a horse, a bird of fire, and even a dancing bear. One ballet was set in a toyshop, another on the beach, and a third — which had music that featured the clacking of a typewriter and the shrill whine of a fire siren — took place outside a circus tent.

In 1929, twenty years after his company's first historic performance in Paris, Diaghilev died and a splendid era of ballet ended suddenly. But while it lasted, the Ballets Russes was a garden for dancers and choreographers, tended and watered by Diaghilev himself. Wherever the scattered seeds of his garden fell, new ballet history took root and flowered.

British ballet grew and flourished after his death thanks to the imagination and hard work of two remarkable women who had danced in his company.

When **Ninette de Valois** joined his troupe in 1923, she had already performed in music-halls and revues, in pantomime, and in two short-lived ballet companies. She had studied ballet with the great Italian teacher, **Enrico Cecchetti**, and attended many performances of the Diaghilev company. But there was only a small audience for classical ballet in England then, and no established company in the country at all.

By the time de Valois left Diaghilev and opened her own school in London, in 1926, she had decided that England needed a ballet company like his, where dancers, designers, composers and choreographers could explore and perfect their art. She shared her idea of a British ballet company with **Lilian Baylis**, the extraordinary manager of the Old Vic theatre. Baylis' first response was to hire de Valois to arrange dances for the theatrical productions and to teach movement to the actors. Five years later, in 1931, she asked de Valois to bring her ballet school to the **Sadler's Wells Theatre** and to start a company there.

The **Vic-Wells Ballet** began as a group of six students plus de Valois. It grew quickly into the **Sadler's Wells Ballet**, which opened its first season at the Royal Opera House, Covent Garden, in 1946, with a brand-new production of *The Sleeping Beauty*. Ten years later, in 1956, the Sadler's Wells Ballet became the **Royal Ballet**. De Valois retired from her position as company director in 1963, after holding it for thirty-two years. But she is still actively involved in the daily activity both of the company and the school that blossomed from her efforts.

The second seed that flowered into British ballet was planted by a young dancer and teacher who, like de Valois, had danced briefly in Diaghilev's company. In 1920, **Marie Rambert** opened her own school in London, where she choreographed little dances for her students and taught them short solos from the Diaghilev repertory. Six years later she started work on a ballet about a dress designer, which was to be performed in a musical revue. Her only male pupil, **Frederick Ashton**, had such original ideas for the piece that he took over its choreography and completed it himself. *A Tragedy of Fashion* marked the beginning of his long, distinguished career as a choreographer. Now Sir Frederick Ashton, he was the first important British choreographer and is one of the greatest choreographers of the twentieth century.

The opening night of *A Tragedy of Fashion* is also considered the first night of Rambert's own company, which is still active today and still called **Ballet Rambert**. In its early years, Rambert invited the greatest dancers of the day to perform on the tiny stage of the **Mercury Theatre** in Notting Hill. Glorious stars of Diaghilev's Ballets Russes — like Karsavina, **Alicia Markova**, **Leon Woizikovsky** and **Anton Dolin** — danced there, as did the young **Margot Fonteyn**.

Rambert made beautiful dancers out of her students, and encouraged young choreographers to make beautiful ballets for them. Ashton and **Antony Tudor** created their earliest masterpieces for Ballet Rambert. And when they left the company, Andrée Howard, Frank Staff and Walter Gore tested their talents with one new ballet after another.

Since Rambert was always eager to stretch the imagination of her dancers and audience, her company became larger and more ambitious over the years. **Norman Morrice**, who is now the director of the Royal Ballet, took over the direction of Ballet Rambert in 1966, and pointed the company toward more modern and experimental ballets. Marie Rambert died in 1982 at the age of 94, but her successful company, now more than fifty years old, continues to represent her lifelong dedication to British ballet.

London's third resident ballet company, the **London Festival Ballet**, grew like a new branch from one of the several touring companies that Alicia Markova and Anton Dolin had formed after Diaghilev died. Markova gave the new company its name in 1950, the year before the Festival of Britain, and danced as its leading ballerina for several years with Dolin, her constant partner. In time, the initial repertory of Russian classics and Fokine revivals expanded to include works by Massine, Tudor and Bournonville. An international group of dancers joined the original handful, and John Gilpin, who inherited Dolin's classical roles, became the company's greatest star.

Today, the Festival Ballet performs regularly in London, on tour throughout Britain, and around the world. The company proudly claims Rudolf Nureyev's production of *Romeo and Juliet*, John Field's *Swan Lake* and Peter Schaufuss' *La Sylphide* among its most popular works.

Ballet in America also got its start from the scattered seeds of Diaghilev's Ballets Russes. The Russian choreographer **George Balanchine** wrote ten ballets in five years for Diaghilev. He then went to America in 1933 at the invitation of **Lincoln Kirstein**, an American writer. With Kirstein's support and backing, Balanchine set out to create a new American style of ballet and a new American company to dance it.

Their first joint creation was the **School of American Ballet**, which they opened in 1933. They organised many small concert groups before the **New York City Ballet** came into existence, in 1948, as a resident company at the New York City Centre theatre. Today, Balanchine's company of over one hundred dancers is ideally trained for the performance of his unique choreography.

16

Like Petipa and Fokine before him, Balanchine reshaped and redefined the classical steps to suit his purposes. The steps he uses need no frills or decoration since many of his ballets have no story or decorative costumes. Instead, the ballets are often a reflection of their music or of the speed and energy of modern life. Almost alone, Balanchine has pushed ballet out of its lavish, courtly habits and into our era of jet planes and gleaming machines. His choreographic originality moved classical ballet into the twentieth century.

Several years after Balanchine arrived in New York, another important ballet company was launched in America. A wealthy dancer named **Lucia Chase** founded **Ballet Theatre** (now **American Ballet Theatre**) in 1939. Her aim was to preserve the best of the old, classical ballets while staging new American ones that would form new styles and traditions. Anton Dolin and Alicia Markova brought the Russian classics with them to Ballet Theatre, Antony Tudor brought his works from Ballet Rambert and quickly choreographed several equally important new ones, and even Michel Fokine joined the new troupe. The company's repertory has always been large and varied, and it still features the colourful early ballets of major American choreographers like **Jerome Robbins** and **Agnes de Mille**.

There are ballet companies all over the world today, and an audience for ballet that numbers in the millions. Ballet is seen on film, on television and as part of musical plays, and dancing has become a profession that commands admiration and respect. The art has survived a long, often difficult history. You can feel proud to be joining the unbroken line of its devoted students.

\*     \*     \*

You will learn a little French as you learn to dance. Each step of the ballet vocabulary has retained the name given to it in the courts of the French kings, early in the seventeenth century.

If you are unsure about the pronunciation of the names, ask a friend or adult who can speak French to read them out to you so you can learn to pronounce them correctly yourself and to recognise them. If you master these terms now, you will be able to walk into a ballet class anywhere in the world and understand the teacher.

# GETTING STARTED

## BASIC REQUIREMENTS FOR THE DANCER

### Posture

What's the very first thing every ballet dancer learns? A step? A jump? No, none of those. Before you can make your first move in ballet, or take even the simplest step across the floor, you must **learn the correct posture for dancing**.

Learning to dance is like building a new house. Unless the foundations of your technique are straight and secure, what you build on top of them will surely collapse, no matter how carefully you build it.

The proper carriage for a dancer is a straight and tall one, with the

**head poised and level on the neck**

**shoulders down**

**back and legs straight**

**stomach and bottom tucked in toward the backbone**

You must carry your weight lightly and let your two legs share it equally, so you are relaxed but always ready to move.

You may think you hold your body that way all the time — it sounds so simple.

But many people poke their bottoms out or their tummies forward without even realising it.

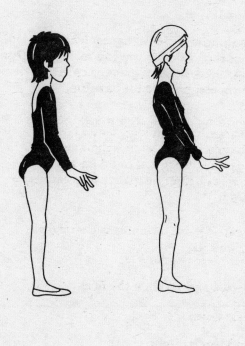

Or they drop all their weight onto one hip and sag like a sack of potatoes.

Don't let **any** sort of sloppy posture creep into your dancing.

Here's one good way to make sure it doesn't.

Turn your side to the mirror
and imagine a straight line —
it's called a **plumb line** —
running from the top of your
head through your ear,
shoulders, hip and knees.

Keep that line in mind and keep it **straight**, even when you're sitting reading a book or walking to school. Erect posture will soon become natural to you, and good posture is the strongest foundation you can possibly build for your dancing.

## Turn-out

Another basic requirement for a good dancer is called **turn-out**. Turn-out is both difficult to achieve and important to maintain, so you must start working for it as soon as you start learning to dance.

You and I tend to stand

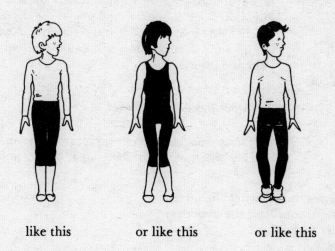

like this          or like this          or like this

with our legs falling into whatever position is most comfortable.

But dancers make a real effort to stand like this:

turning each leg out, away from the other, as if trying to place them back to back.

**Turn-out starts in the hip socket and continues all the way down to the ground.**

You must **never** turn out either your feet or your knees without at least trying to turn out your thigh and hip as well. You'll want to do so at first, because your foot pivots so much more easily at the ankle than your whole leg does at the hip. But your legs would twist like corkscrews if you danced with your knees pointing forward and your feet pointing in opposite directions, one to the left and one to the right. Ouch! Don't even try it for fun — it's not! And in the end, that position will cause you only pain and injuries.

Turn-out has two purposes:

It allows you to move your leg freely and quickly wherever your dancing takes it, and

It gives the audience the nicest view of your legs, the smooth front surface

rather than
the lumpy, bumpy
side.

Turn-out is so important to good dancing that it needs constant attention.

Luckily, you can work on it while you're doing something else. The next time you're waiting for a bus, you can secretly do this:

> Stand up straight, tuck in your tummy and bottom, put your heels together, and point your toes slightly away from each other. Then try to turn your legs back to back. Use the big muscles in your bottom and the long ones on the inside of your thighs. Tighten the big ones, and push out and around with the long ones in your legs.

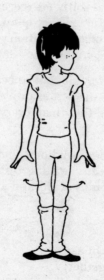

No one but you will know how hard you're working. And if you continue to practise, slowly but surely you'll develop the turn-out you need to dance properly and gracefully.

# Line

A third basic element for a dancer's technique is very easy to talk about, but much harder for you to create when you dance. That important element is called **line**.

Don't be fooled. It has nothing to do with straight lines. Straight lines are for stick figures and that's the last thing you want to look like.

In classical dancing, line is simply the attractive and balanced arrangement of the various parts of your body. Whether you're moving or standing still, you have to know where all the bits of you actually are — both in relation to each other and to the space around you. You can make yourself look as sturdy and tall as a tree, or as softly curved as a swan's neck. But unless you're very careful, a sharp elbow or a floppy foot can easily ruin the beauty of your position.

You can't do exercises for line, but you can study it by looking for it. Nature provides the best examples, and once you start to look for them, you'll find them everywhere.

Look around your own home and your garden. Look at the steam swirling up from the tea-kettle, or the spirals of frost on a windowpane.

Notice how the petals of a
flower fit smoothly together,
without crowding each other,

and how the wings of a soaring sparrow curve on either side of its body.

Watch a cat jump off a table or curl up to sleep in the sun.

**Nothing is out of place or left to chance. That's how you must learn to dance.**

When you look at nature, you're studying another secret about ballet dancing without even realising it.

Did you ever see a cabbage forcing its way out of the ground, or a rosebud rushing into bloom? Does a dog huff and puff after a sprint across the yard? Does a cat wrinkle up its face with concentration as it picks its way delicately along a fence? No, of course not — and neither does a dancer.

All good dancing looks easy, and the very best dancing looks absolutely effortless. So while you're trying to learn the proper posture for dancing, trying to let a graceful line flow from the top of your head to the tips of your fingers and toes,

you must also try to smile and relax.

Eventually your dancing will both look and feel natural, but only if you make all the strain and effort of doing it invisible.

Is dancing starting to sound like hard work, with lots of rules to remember —

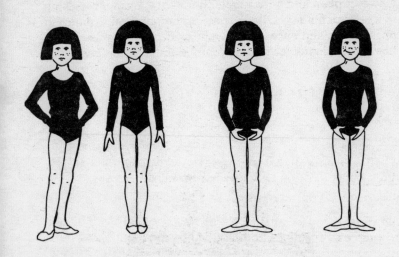

stand up straight,          turn out,          relax and smile?

Well, it **is** hard work. It's very hard indeed to make difficult things look simple. But some day there may be many, many people watching you dance. And it is the grace and beauty of your movements and the practised ease of your performance that will make you a pleasure to watch.

# SURROUNDINGS AND EQUIPMENT

However plain and bare a ballet studio may seem, everything in it is there for a specific purpose: to prepare you to dance in front of an audience. You don't need red velvet curtains, blazing spotlights, or pretty costumes to learn to dance.

You don't even need a real stage. And you may have decided to study ballet for fun, without thinking ahead to a professional career at all. But ballet is a **performance art** — not a competitive sport or a game — so learning to present yourself to an audience is a major part of learning to dance.

There is no live audience in the classroom except for your teacher, but there should always be a **mirror**. In a way, the mirror replaces the audience. It sits in front of your dancing and watches it. Watching yourself in the mirror is the only way you'll ever see what an audience sees, so watch closely and pay attention.

29

Do you see a little ballerina
or a princely danseur
when you look at yourself?

If you do, you're probably looking into your imagination and seeing the dancer you want to become. The mirror actually shows you the dancer you **are**, at each moment, and that reflection is much more important. It will show you exactly when your elbow is poking out or when your foot is dangling like a wet rag instead of pointing neatly — just the things your imagination won't notice!

If you let it, the mirror will be your friend and guide. Every studio has a large one, if not an entire wall of mirrors. When you practise your ballet at home, between lessons, try to stand in front of a large or full-length mirror. A mirror that shows you only one arm or leg at a time won't help you very much. Your body doesn't dance in sections — all of you dances all at once.

# Clothing

In order to see yourself clearly, move easily, and keep your muscles warm, you should wear clean, tight-fitting practice clothes whenever you dance. Both boys and girls wear **tights** — girls' tights cover the feet, but boys will need lightweight socks — and soft leather **ballet slippers**, with a strip of elastic sewn across each one to keep it firmly on your foot. Girls should wear **leotards**, with long or short sleeves, over their tights, and boys should wear **T-shirts**, tucked neatly into the waistband of their tights.

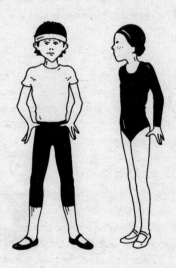

Even your hair must be under control. If it's long enough to flop, get it out of your eyes and out of the way. Girls can make plaits or pony tails and pin them up off the neck. Boys can always wear a tennis headband or even tie a handkerchief around their forehead to control the fringe.

## Floor Surface

The best surface for dancing is a clean smooth floor. Most ballet studios have wooden ones, and you'll notice that they're **never** polished. That's because wax can make a floor as slippery as ice, and just as unsafe to dance on.

Before you begin practising at home, go on a treasure hunt. See if you can find a floor like the one in your ballet studio. Waxed linoleum will be too slippery, jumping on concrete will rattle your bones, and turning on grass or thick carpet will tangle your toes. A good floor is neither too slick, too rough, or too bumpy. It may be hard to find, but it's worth the hunt.

A smooth clean floor will feel like a magic carpet under your feet.

# Music

Now think for a minute about the last ballet you saw. Did you only **see** it?

No, you probably heard music with it too.

One of the joys of dancing is moving to many different musical tunes and rhythms. Your teacher will provide either records or a pianist to accompany your class, and you'll find the music gives you energy and carries you along when you're tired. At home, you can sing to yourself while you practise, or play your own records or radio, or even just clap your hands.

Music sets the rhythm and speed for your movements, so the music you choose to dance to will make important demands on your body. When you walk to the rhythm of a marching band, you tend to step quickly and lightly to keep time with it. If the band plays slower, you'll take longer strides to keep in step.

You'll have to move both quickly **and** slowly as a dancer. You can make a game of learning to do both by trying to repeat the same movement — a kick or a little hop — to faster and faster music. But remember that **nothing should ever be left out or slurred over**. The best dancer is the one who executes all the steps and positions neatly and accurately, no matter how quickly he must do them.

Fitting your body to the music is a wonderful puzzle that's part of the fun of dancing. The closer you can make them fit together, the better the dancer you'll become.

## The *barre*

The last requirement for practicing is something that you'll use in every ballet class throughout your life, but it will never go on stage with you. It's called a *barre*. In the studio, the barre is a thick wooden pole that's bolted to the wall at waist height. At home, you can use almost anything as a barre:

> the back of a chair,
> the edge of a table,
> the top of a garden
> fence, even a
> doorknob

as long as you can comfortably rest one hand on it without either leaning down or reaching up.

> A dancer **never leans on the barre**
> **never holds it really tightly**
> **never pulls away from it.**

You must learn to hold yourself up with your own muscles, whether you're standing on one leg or two, flat on your feet or balanced on the balls of your feet in **relevé**. The barre is there to help you and guide you, like a good friend. But everything you first learn to do at the barre, you will soon be doing in the centre of the room, just as if you were on a stage. You will support your own body, move different parts of it easily through space, and adjust the speed and direction of your movement — and there will be nothing to hold you up.

> While you're working to develop your strength
> and flexibility at the barre, you must also learn
> to do without it.

# BASIC POSITIONS OF THE FEET AND ARMS

**Now** you can begin to dance, and ballet dancing begins with standing still. Before you learn to move, you must learn to stand in certain positions that every student around the world learns.

## Feet

There are five positions of the feet and they look like this:

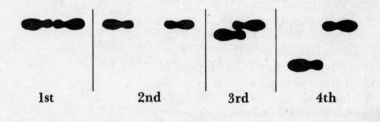

1st          2nd          3rd          4th

5th

Every step you learn will begin and end in one of those five positions.

You could say that correct posture is the strong foundation for your dancing, and the five positions of the feet are the ground floor on which everything else will be built. In all five of them, your back and knees should be kept straight, head level, shoulders down, and bottom and stomach tucked in under your ribs.

**1st position** is the easiest. Simply put your heels together and point your toes away from each other. But remember: each knee must point in the same direction as the foot underneath it. So don't turn out your feet any further than you can turn out your knee and thigh and entire leg.

1

**2nd position** isn't much harder. It's just 1st position with a space between your heels. To find the correct length of that space for your body, slide one foot sideways, away from 1st position, until only your toes are still touching the floor. When you can't reach any further sideways, lower your heel again. That's **your** 2nd position.

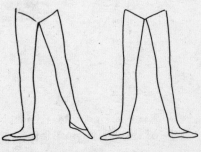

2

For **3rd position**, bring your feet
together again but let them overlap, so
the heel of one nestles right against the
arch of the other. 3rd position is rarely
used in dancing, but you should learn
it just the same.

**3**

You find your **4th position** exactly the
same way you found your 2nd
position. Start in 1st and again slide
one foot away, but this time slide it in
front of you. It should go just as far as
you can easily reach without putting
any weight on it. When you put your
heel down again, your front foot and
leg should be just as turned out as they
were in 1st position.

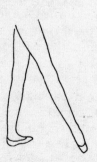

**4**

**5th position**, the last one, is a bit tricky. Go back to 1st again. Glide one foot in front of the other until it reaches third position and then keep on moving it in the same direction until the heel of the moving foot nearly reaches the big toe of your standing foot.

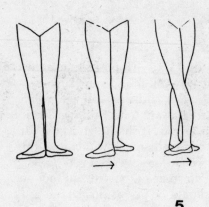

**5**

The crisscross you've made is 5th position. The tricky bit is that your straight and turned-out legs must crisscross too if your feet are ever going to form this position.

Don't worry if you can't quite touch big toe to opposite heel at first. It will become easier with practice, as your turn-out improves and your muscles grow longer and stronger. A modified 5th position is fine to begin with, as long as you continue to aim for the proper finished position.

## Arms

Now, where will you put your arms? They can't simply hang down at your sides like limp spaghetti or stick out like hedgehog quills. Here are the four positions you will use most often:

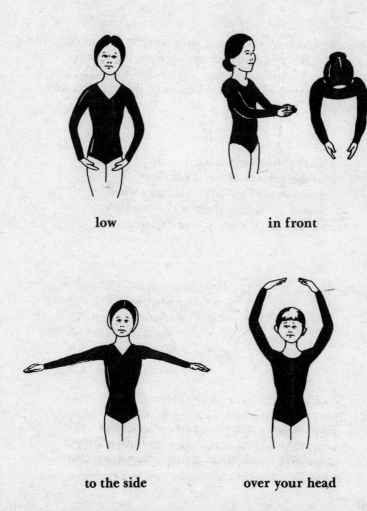

low                        in front

to the side              over your head

As you make each of these positions, pretend you're holding a giant soap bubble in your arms. That will remind you to relax your arms, neck and shoulders, because you know that you wouldn't need any strength or muscle tension to carry a bubble. And the slightest edge or sharp point would pop it, so curve your arms very gently at the elbow and wrist, and smooth all the corners out of them.

Wherever you hold your arms, your fingers should continue and extend the nice line they make. Even your fingers must seem relaxed when you dance. Your hand won't fall into a pleasant position all by itself. You must put it there, and here's how:

Shake your fingers hard, as if you were shaking drops of water off them. The position they fall into naturally when you stop shaking them is the one they should be in when you're dancing.

Keep a sharp eye for strays — any finger that jabs out can burst that imaginary bubble in your arms and break their gentle line at the same time.

## Your Body

As soon as you've learned the five positions, you should start thinking of your body in the terms professional dancers use. Here are several important ones:

> The leg you are moving is always referred to as the **working leg**. The other leg, the one holding you up, is called the **supporting leg**. Of course, when you're standing still on both feet, **both** legs support you equally. But you can't take a step on a foot that's already carrying your weight. The minute you shift your weight off two legs, one becomes the worker and the other becomes the supporter.

Where you place your weight and how you find your balance are problems that need solving every single time you take a step or change your position.

You solve these problems in two ways:

by placing your weight properly, or centring it, and by pulling it up off the ground, using both your mind and your muscles.

41

Oh yes, mental effort will help you as much as physical effort when you dance. Use them both!

You've probably been **centring** your body all your life without even knowing it. If you stand in 1st position, with a plumb line running right down to your heels, your weight is naturally balanced over both feet.

But where is your weight in 2nd position? Remember, you've only moved one leg — and nothing else — to get there. Your back and legs are still straight, and neither hip is jutting up. If you're still carrying your weight equally on both legs, as you should be, you've already got it perfectly centred over the space between your feet.

See how easy it is.

**Pulling up** your weight is just the same as pulling up your socks.

Gravity and the laws of nature cause everything to fall down unless someone or something holds it up.

Elastic holds your socks up. Without it, they fall down around your ankles.

Your muscles hold your arm up. Without them, you couldn't lift it from your side.

And your thought and concentration hold your muscles and your weight up.

Just think how you move when you're tired — all droopy and dragging, more like an elephant really than a dancer.

Dancing is the opposite of drooping. When you pull up, it's as if you're fighting sleep and fighting gravity. You don't hold your breath or lift your shoulders or tighten any muscles to pull up — quite the reverse. Pulling up really means thinking up and feeling alert, relaxed but ready to move in any direction at any speed.

# AT THE BARRE

## WARMING UP

A dancer is like a delicate instrument and a strong machine all at the same time. While you've been working to turn out, pull up, centre your weight, and master the basic positions of the feet, you've been tuning up the instrument. Now you've got to start warming up the machine.

All warm-up steps, from the slowest and simplest to the most energetic and intricate, are practised at the barre. Rest one hand **lightly** on it, and make your own muscles do the job of keeping you properly placed and balanced. The less you lean on the barre now, the easier it will be for you to let go of it later, when you want to walk away from it and dance in the centre of the room.

Dancers all over the world perform the same arm movements before they begin each exercise at the barre. There are only two movements and they're very simple:

On count 1, raise the arm that is not connecting you to the barre so it's curved in front of you.

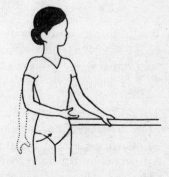

On count 2, open that arm to 2nd position, to the side, where you should hold it until you've finished the exercise.

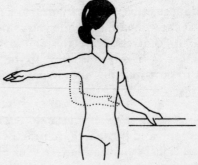

These two movements together are called a **preparation**.

When you complete your preparation, your arms will be in identical positions on either side of your body. Holding them there should help you find your balance. And once you're balanced, you're well prepared to dance.

Wouldn't it be dull if you could only dance with one side of your body? Both sides of your body are equally important to your dancing, and you must train them both with equal care.

Therefore, every step or combination of steps must be practised *twice*, once with the left hand on the barre and again with the right hand on the barre. The leg that is furthest from the barre naturally has more room to move.

So when your left hand is on the barre, your right leg is the working leg.

And when your right hand is on the barre, your left leg is the working leg.

Does that seem complicated? I'm sure you understand the importance of practising every movement to both sides. Once you begin to work at the barre, turning around to repeat each exercise to the other side will become automatic.

47

# Warm-up positions

Modern dancers and gymnasts perform standing, sitting, or lying down, but all ballet dancing takes place while you're standing. So your feet, ankles and legs — which never rest while you're dancing — will need warming up before anything else.

## *Demi-plié* (half bend)

Stand in 1st position at the barre with one hand resting lightly on it, and perform a preparation with the other arm. Then bend your knees out over your toes just as far as you can without lifting your heels.

Take two counts to bend your legs and another two counts to straighten them.

This little bend should be done four times, slowly and carefully, in **1st, 2nd, 4th** and **5th position**. And don't forget to turn around and do them with your other hand on the barre. Check these points in each position:

Are your knees directly over your toes?
They will be if you're turned out.

Are your heels pressing down into the floor?

Are you pulling your weight up even as you let your body down? You must never sit or squat in a plié, and you won't be doing either one if you're pulled up.

*Grand plié* (big bend) follows demi-plié in your warm-up, and stretches the muscles on the front and back of your legs even further.

Stand in 1st position, one hand on the barre, and count to four. On counts 1 and 2, execute a demi-plié — knees over toes, heels down, bottom under you and back straight. Then as you count 3 and 4, push your knees out even further over your toes and lower your bottom towards the floor as they go.

Don't let your heels come off the floor until you have to. When they do, push your knees open even wider, so your bottom is right down near them and you look like a frog.

Take another four counts to reverse the movement and return to a standing position. For the best stretch, **put your heels back down the floor as soon as you can** — certainly by count 6 and well before you've straightened your legs completely.

Repeat grand plié twice in 1st, 2nd, 4th and 5th position, and then put your other hand on the barre and repeat the entire sequence.

Your muscles will develop length and strength if you control them. Pull up every time you sink down, then push your heels down as your body rises up. Ballet dancing is a fight against gravity, and the fight starts here, with your first pliés at the barre.

## Relevé

In plié you stretch your muscles by bending your legs.

You can also stretch the opposite way, by straightening your legs and pulling up so that you actually pull your heels off the floor. Rolling your weight forward and up onto the balls of your feet is called a *relevé* in ballet. Once you're in that position, balanced on half-pointe or what's called ***demi-pointe,*** you should feel as if your whole body would float up to the ceiling — exactly like a balloon — if your toes weren't sticking you to the ground.

Relevé stretches your feet and ankles, and it also helps you find and hold your balance. Stand in 1st position facing the barre with both hands resting on it. Pulling up all the muscles in the back of your legs and in your bottom, take two counts to raise your heels and another two counts to lower them.

Repeat that four times and lift your hands off the barre as you rise into relevé the fourth time, so that you are balanced on the balls of your feet.

You won't have to worry about balancing on demi-pointe if you learn a little mental trick:

**Never think of your weight as plopped down flat on your foot.**

**Instead, think of it as poised lightly on three spots.**

When you relevé, all you do is lift the spot beneath your heel off the floor. The two spots beneath the widest part of your foot are still firmly pinned to the ground and your body can rest gently and easily on them.

Another trick is to pretend a
string is tacked to the middle
to your chest. You won't have
to push your body up into
relevé if you imagine a light
tug on the string lifting your
weight as you lift your heels.

Practise relevé after your second demi-plié in each position,
and remember to hold yourself up with long, strong leg
muscles and not with the barre. You'll know you're doing the
work yourself when you can let go of the barre, stand on demi-
pointe, and not lose your balance.

You can also practise relevé any time you're waiting for
something, whether you're beside the bathtub or in a queue
at the cinema. Use the sink or a railing as your barre, place
yourself properly in 1st or 2nd position, and then float your
heels up and try to let go and balance. Are your legs still
turned out from the hip? Are your shoulders relaxed? You
can't lift yourself by your collarbone or by holding your
breath. Just think tall and float up!

## Port de bras

**Port de bras** means carriage of the arms, but it also stands for
all the graceful, flowing ways you can move your body,
shoulders and head. At the barre, you can do a different set of
bending and stretching movements, a different port de bras,
with each position of the feet. Do each of these sequences once
after your grands pliés to warm and loosen the muscles in your
back, shoulders, stomach, and all around your waist.

**After grand plié in 1st position**, bend forward from the waist and lower your head toward your straight knees. At the same time, drop your free arm toward the floor.

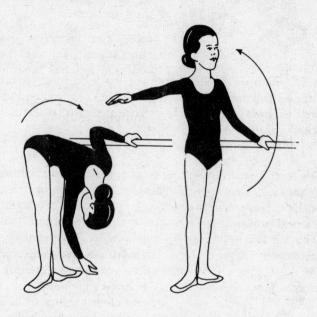

Make your back very long and your neck very loose to give your backbone a good stretch. Then straighten up as if your waist were a hinge. Move everything above it smoothly, as one unit, until your torso, shoulders, neck and head are back in place and lined up over your hips.

**In 2nd position**, carry your free arm up over your head and then let it push your head and chest toward the barre so the shoulder nearest the barre dips towards it.

Keep your face front, your hips square, and your weight over the space between your feet. Then reverse the movement and return to an upright position.

**In 4th position**, curve your free arm over your head again, but this time bend arm, head and chest backwards as far as you can without toppling over.

Then return to a straight posture. You may not be able to bend very far at first, but do **not** poke your tummy forward in order to bend back further. Practise will give you all the flexibility you need.

**In 5th position**, still using your waist as a hinge or pivot, try to move your upper body in an entire circle. Bend forward first, then towards the barre, lean back, and finally reach away from the barre.

Your legs, bottom and hips must stay straight and firm as a treetrunk, no matter which way you bend and stretch the branches of your arms.

Count eight, not too slowly, for **each** port de bras. Use four counts to bend your body and four to straighten it. You'll need two counts of eight for the full circle in 5th position. And remember to do all these stretches after your grands pliés to both sides. Every bit of you should be warm when you finish.

# STRETCHING YOUR FEET AND LEGS

You've performed all the warming up steps so far while standing on two feet. It's time now to begin stretching and strengthening each leg and foot in turn.

When you learned to move from 1st to 2nd position, and from 3rd to 4th, you were also learning *battement tendu*, even though you didn't know its name. Tendu means stretched — a battement tendu stretches your foot and leg. It also improves your turn-out and gives you practice in shifting your centred weight from two legs to one.

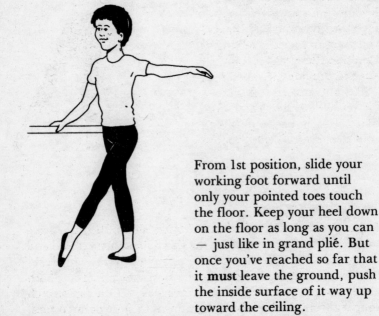

From 1st position, slide your working foot forward until only your pointed toes touch the floor. Keep your heel down on the floor as long as you can — just like in grand plié. But once you've reached so far that it **must** leave the ground, push the inside surface of it way up toward the ceiling.

This will force your whole leg to turn out right up to your hip socket. Take two counts to extend the foot and two more counts to return it to 1st position.

Tendu to the side is exactly the same, a slow stretch, but now your heel will stay directly beneath your foot. If you could look straight down from above at the extended foot, you wouldn't see the heel at all.

Turning out while you tendu to the back is especially hard because your knee will want to face the floor and your heel will want to face the ceiling. Don't let them! Keep your knee to the side — you can pull it outward by using those big muscles in your thighs and bottom — and keep pushing your heel down toward the floor.

Repeat your tendus twice to the front, twice to the side, twice to the back and twice again to the side. Then turn around and let your other leg be the working leg for the entire sequence. Begin and end every tendu in 1st position, and keep both knees straight the whole time. That way, tendu can stretch your leg from the hip all the way down to your pointed toes.

If you **insert a demi-plié after each tendu**, you'll stretch your leg muscles even further. Try it. Do the entire tendu exercise just as you did it the first time. But each time you return your foot to first position and transfer your weight from the one supporting leg back onto two legs, bend your knees out over your toes in demi-plié.

The next tendu will begin from this demi-plié position; the supporting leg will straighten beneath you at exactly the same time that the working leg slides out into tendu.

Now you're stretching your legs twice in one exercise.

In plié you stretch them as far as they'll go with your heels down, and in tendu you stretch your working leg as far as it will go with its heel up. The two stretches together should make your legs feel warm, pliable, and ready to move in any direction — the way a toffee feels under your tongue.

# BRUSHING MOVEMENTS: PREPARING TO JUMP

## Battement dégagé

Another kind of battement, **battement dégagé**, requires greater speed and accuracy and much more energy than tendu. Dégagé is a fast, sharp movement, as snappy as a rubber band.

To do it, your working foot has to brush out from its starting position, in either 1st or 5th position,

through tendu, and

right off the ground.

You shouldn't lift your leg very high or hold it in the air very long, but you won't have time to if you make your dégagé short and sharp.

From 5th position, do four clear dégagés in each direction — front, side, back and side. Brush your foot off the floor with real strength each time, as if it were a rocket launching your leg into the air, and then snap it back into position sharply.

Make sure your legs stay absolutely straight and that you finish each dégagé in a good, tight 5th position with **both** heels on the floor. Count the exercise like this:

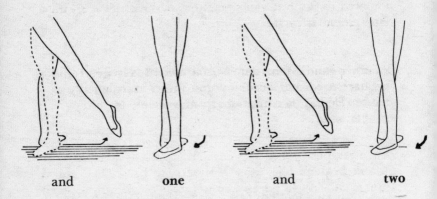

| and | **one** | and | **two** |

That will keep lazy legs from drifting aimlessly in the air.

When you dégagé to the side, you should alternate 5th position each time you close your working leg. That means your working foot should close

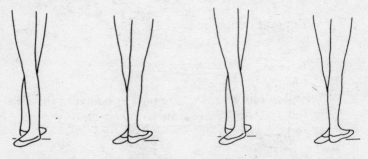

| in 5th position front | then in back | then in front | then in back |

to be in the proper place to begin dégagé to the back.

How would you alternate 5th positions if you wanted to follow four dégagés to the side with four more to the front?

**Dégagé is a basic preparation for jumping.** You'll need both the upward whoosh of the leg and the neat 5th position it closes in when you learn to jump. And you'll be even better prepared to jump if you sometimes practise dégagé with a demi-plié after each one.

Here's why. **Every jump begins and ends in demi-plié.**
That's one of the most important rules of ballet.
The rule has **no** exceptions.

When you push your knees out and your heels down into the ground in demi-plié, your legs become like tightly coiled springs. When you release those springs by giving yourself a good push off the floor with your heels and straightening your knees, you'll pop into the air like a jack-in-the-box.

Dégagés with demi-plié will let you practice jumping without actually leaving the floor. Try a series of them — two front, two side, two back, and two side — and you'll see what I mean.

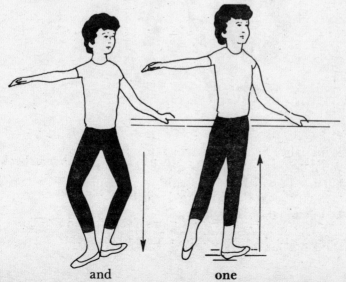

and                     one                     61

## Echappé

*Echappé* is another jump you can practise at the barre.

Stand in 5th position, right foot front, resting both hands lightly on the barre. Demi-plié for your preparation and then, with a little spring, shoot both feet away from you at once.

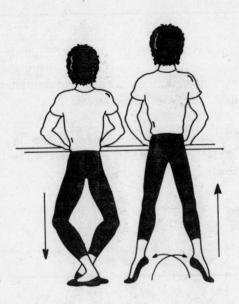

When they're fully stretched to either side, you'll be standing in 2nd position and in relevé balanced on demi-pointe with your weight still centred between your outstretched legs. Your legs should flash open like the blades of a pair of scissors. Echappé means escape, so you should think of your feet as escaping from each other.

Finish the step by flashing your legs together again. You should end as you began, in 5th position and in demi-plié, only now your left foot should be in front.

To build up your strength and put a nice springy feeling into your legs, do eight échappés, one after the other, alternating 5th position each time you close your feet. Count quickly and sharply:

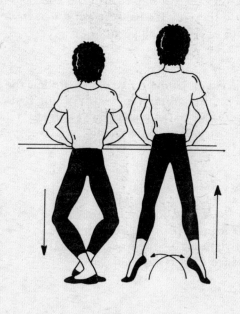

and      **one**

and      **two**

# CIRCULAR MOVEMENTS:

## To Free Your Hips and Improve Your Balance

### *Rond de Jambe*

In all the exercises so far, you've carried your legs only along straight paths, either to the front, side, or back of you. But if you can move your body in curves and circles, as you did in port de bras, isn't there a step that moves your legs that way too? Of course there is. It's called a *rond de jambe*, which literally means a round of the leg.

Executing a rond de jambe is like playing follow the dots. In one smooth, continuous motion, your working foot connects the front, side and back points you've already touched in tendu with all the points in between.

Look at the shape of the movement first. If your left hand is on the barre and your left leg is supporting all your weight, your right leg — the working leg — moves from 1st position like this:

Completely turned out, with the toes pointed and the knee very straight, it reaches forward in tendu, then continues around to the side — still turned out — then to the back, and finally returns to 1st position.

You can do exactly the same movement in reverse, reaching straight behind you to start, and then to the side and front before closing again in 1st position.

As long as your leg moves freely and easily from your hip socket, like the leg of a compass, rond de jambe will help you develop the flexibility and fluidity that every dancer needs. And remember, the movement is **impossible** if you're putting any weight at all on the working leg. How can you move a leg if you're leaning your weight on it?

At first, you might want to practise half a rond de jambe at a time.

From 1st position, tendu front on count 1, rond de jambe to the side on counts 2 and 3, and close to 1st on count 4.

Repeat four times. Then reverse it: tendu back on 1, carry side on 2 and 3, close on 4.

Repeat that four times. Then turn around, and do it all over again with your other hand on the barre.

Once you're comfortable with that, try eight full ronds de jambe in a row. As soon as you do more than one, you'll discover the second continuous movement in the step.

The first was the movement that made the semi-circle.

The second connects the ends of the semi-circle by passing through 1st position without actually stopping in it. It's hard to keep your balance while your working leg keeps moving around you. Stand straight, turn out, and follow the dots. A waltz count of three will guide you to the right flow and phrasing for an entire rond de jambe sequence. Count 1 for each connecting movement, and count 2, 3 for each semi-circle.

66

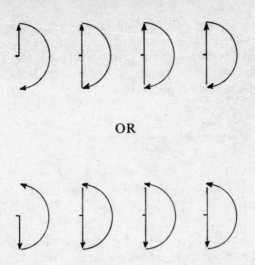

OR

Rond de jambe is difficult. You can be proud of yourself when you make it flow smoothly.

While you're resting from the struggle with rond de jambe, you can learn the proper terms for the directions in which you've been doing it.

An *en dehors* — outward — movement is a circular one that progresses from front to back, like the eight ronds de jambe that began with a tendu to the front. It's easy to remember if you think of that working leg moving **out** of sight as it travels around to the back.

An *en dedans* — inward — movement is a circular one that progresses from back to front. As you did each of the eight ronds de jambe that started with tendu back, your working leg moved **into** your field of vision.

Are you ready for a little more French and a new rond de jambe? All the ones you've done until now have been performed *à terre* — on the ground. There is also a rond de jambe *en l'air* — in the air — but it takes strength, skill, and precision to do it properly.

The two new elements in the step are these:

1.  Your leg is now off the ground, lifted in 2nd position.

2.  Only **part** of your leg, the part from your knee to your toe, makes the circle. Once the leg is raised into position, only that lower part of it should move.

The rond de jambe is now: shaped like this

It's a complete circle instead of half of one.

It's made by half your leg instead of all of it.

Try it from 5th position, right foot front. Dégagé side so your working leg is just a few centimetres off the floor. Wherever you lift it at first is where it must remain for the whole exercise, so don't kick it way up when you dégagé.

Lock your thigh into place, break the straight line of your leg at your knee, and try to draw a circle in the air with your foot. Actually, you'll only be able to draw an oval or a flattened circle. Your foot will move slightly behind your thigh, in to touch your knee, slightly in front of your thigh, and back out to 2nd position en l'air.

Then close your leg in 5th behind. You'll need eight counts: two for the dégagé, two to circle in towards the knee, two to complete the circle outwards, and two to close your foot gently in 5th position back.

Try it again. Dégagé from 5th position back, fix your leg securely in space, and do an en dedans rond de jambe. After the dégagé, your stretched foot will move into your vision just slightly in front of your extended thigh. It will then come in to touch your knee, continue its circle slightly behind your thigh, and return to 2nd position en l'air before closing gently in 5th position front.

**Rond de jambe en l'air** is quite an advanced movement. You'll eventually be able to do it much faster and with your leg much higher, but for now, use the step to test your balance, placement and turn-out.

*   *   *

Are you leaning hard on the barre or pulling away from it?

Is there still a plumb line running down to your heels?

Are you turning out with the big muscles in your bottom and thighs?

Is your tummy tucked in?

Is your arm gracefully curved to the side?

Are you still smiling?

*   *   *

# PREPARING TO BEAT

Do you begin to see how ballet is put together? Its airy delicacy rests on the rock-solid support of practice and common sense.

Perfecting one movement prepares you to learn the next, and different movements often tie up together as neatly and tightly as knitting.

## *Frappé*

For *frappé*, one of the small battements, you'll need to tie three things together:

the outward force of **dégagé**

the isolated use of the lower leg that you learned for **rond de jambe**, and

a completely new position

In dégagé, the working foot starts out flat on the floor, either in 1st or 5th position. But frappé means **struck**: your working foot has to strike the floor as it moves away from you, so it must be off the floor before it starts that movement. The new position's name tells you where to put that foot when you lift it off the floor to begin a frappé.

## Sur le cou de pied

The new position is called *sur le cou de pied*, which means on the neck of the foot. What is the neck of the foot? Why, the ankle, of course!

Wrap one foot snugly around the other ankle, with your heel in front of the supporting leg and your toes tucked around behind it.

Once you've bent your working knee like that and taken your weight off it, it's much easier to turn it out to the side. Each time you frappé, you should stretch and fold the lower part of your leg like an accordian while holding that turn-out with the upper part.

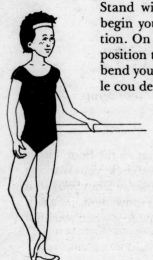

Stand with your left hand on the barre and begin your frappés with a two count preparation. On count 1, slide your right foot from 5th position to tendu in 2nd position. On count 2, bend your working knee and place your foot sur le cou de pied.

At the same time, carry your arm from the side to a low position, fingers curved toward your body, where you'll hold it for the entire exercise.

The accent or force of frappé is always **outward**, and the ball of your foot must strike the floor each time it flies out. Count the movement like this: (preparation) one, two . . .

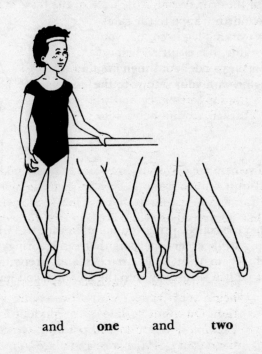

and        **one**        and        **two**

An entire frappé sequence would include four frappés in each direction — front, side, back and side.

You'll have to make a small adjustment halfway through this sequence. You can't possibly frappé to the back if your working leg is sur le cou de pied in front, because your supporting leg would be in the way.

The way around this little problem is simply to move your cou de pied position around to the back of your ankle.

After the fourth frappé to the side, fold your working leg in so that your entire working foot is curled behind the supporting ankle. And then off you go again with your frappé to the back.

Remember the coiled spring you found in your legs while you were doing dégagé? Frappé puts that same springy feeling into each leg in turn as it stretches and strengthens the muscles that will thrust you into the air when you jump.

Your ability to jump high — properly called your **elevation** — is not always the most important thing in ballet. Some small jumps are meant to be performed very close to the floor and very quickly, with a sparkle that makes them special. The sparkle comes from you, specifically from your beating your legs together or rearranging them while you're in the air. You can start **learning how to beat** while you're at the barre, even though you won't actually jump until later in the class.

## Petit Battement

The movement to practice for a sparkly jump is called *petit battement*. And the basis for petit battement is the sur le cou de pied position you've just learned. Any battement is a beating movement of the leg, and petit simply means little. So petits battements are literally very small beats, which your working foot performs against your ankle.

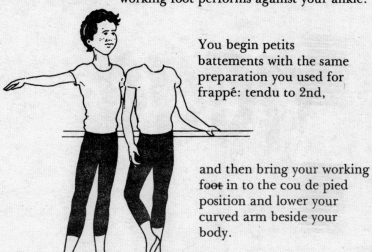

You begin petits battements with the same preparation you used for frappé: tendu to 2nd,

and then bring your working foot in to the cou de pied position and lower your curved arm beside your body.

Now all you have to do in petit battement is swing your lower leg out from the knee, just far enough to change your cou de pied position from the front of your ankle to the back. Swing your leg out again, and slip your working foot back in front. Swing out, beat back. Swing out, beat front.

From your hip to your knee, your leg is completely still and as turned out as you can make it without moving it, exactly as in frappé. Your lower leg and pointed foot swing from the hinge of your knee, slowly and gently at first, and then with stronger accents and greater speed as the movement becomes more comfortable for you.

At first, do eight petits battements on each leg, counting slowly and evenly, like this:

and     one     and     two

Then change the accent and increase the speed. As you say "and," slip your foot completely around your ankle. As you say "one," bring it back again to its starting position with a good strong slap:

| either | back | **front** | back | **front** | |
|--------|------|-----------|------|-----------|------------|
|        | and  | **1**     | and  | **2**     | right up to 8, |

| or | front | **back** | front | **back** | |
|----|-------|----------|-------|----------|--------|
|    | and   | **1**    | and   | **2**    | up to 8. |

Finally, place your foot in cou de pied front and begin to count slowly to sixteen. While you're counting, do as many petits battements as you can. Make sure that nothing moves but the lower part of your leg, and that each cou de pied position, front and back, is neat and accurate.

**Sloppy petits battements at the barre will make you a sloppy jumper later.**

**Quick, precise petits battements will make you sparkle.**

After you've got the hang of petit battement, you can practise these same exercises on **demi-pointe**. Whenever you do, let go of the barre at the end of each sequence and find your balance with your working foot held in cou de pied. If you're poised and pulled up, you won't have to hunt very long for a balanced position.

All together, the quick, lively steps in ballet — jumps, beats, turns, and connecting steps — are called **allegro** movements. When you leave the barre to dance in the centre of the floor, you'll need to move lightly and precisely in your allegro dancing, clearly showing the audience every change of your body's direction and every tiny twinkle of your feet.

# ADAGIO

Adagio movements, in contrast to allegro ones, are slow, sustained and flowing. The dancer must stand firmly in one spot for adagio, and on one leg as well, moving the other leg and the arms, head and torso through one graceful pose after another. **Adagio dancing calls for line, balance, strength in the back and legs, and flexibility in the torso.**

That may sound very demanding, but by now you should be used to standing strongly and securely on one leg while the other is moving. If the barre is still holding you up, you're surely headed for trouble when you have to stand without it in the centre of the floor. Before that moment comes, let's learn a few adagio movements. Put all the flash and sparkle of petits battements out of your mind: make your body long, lithe and silvery instead.

## *Passé*

*Passé* can be performed by itself, but it's used more often as a linking movement in adagio. Your working leg travels through this position on its way somewhere else, so you can think of passé as a passageway between more important movements.

Can you shape the number four with your legs?

You can't make a ⏘ but you can make a 4

That's exactly the position of your legs in passé. Here's how you get there:

Raise your working foot from 5th position — heel first, ball and toe following after — and slide it up your supporting leg until your pointed toes are just touching the knee opposite them.

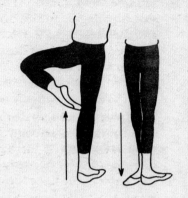

Then slide that foot down your leg again and close it in 5th position back.

That's it. That's all there is to it.

You can practise passé at different speeds. First do four passés slowly, giving four slow counts to each one — two counts to slide your foot to your knee, and the next two counts to slide it back to the floor. Alternate 5th position, closing back, front, back, front.

Then do four more passés, allowing only two counts for each one. On the first count, snap your working foot into the passé position. On the second count, snap it back down to 5th.

You might even want to do a second four passés at this speed, adding a relevé on your supporting foot each time your working foot flips up to your knee. But no matter how quickly you count, make sure you pass through all the same positions at the faster speed that you passed through at the original slow tempo.

Keep your knee well turned out, make a perfect

4

and you'll have a perfect passé.

A linked series of different steps is called an *enchaînement* in ballet. Passé provides a beginning for an adagio enchaînement, like an introduction or an overture. Once your pointed toes have reached the passé position, alongside your supporting knee, your leg can unfold in any direction at all.

## Développé

Wherever you decide to place that leg, the act of unfolding it, straightening it out, and holding it in the air, is called *développé*. Développé is often the largest movement of an entire adagio sequence, and the most exciting one for the audience because it will seem completely effortless. To give that impression, you must have total control of every part of your body. You must hold your balance without wobbling, move your leg smoothly and continuously, and place it precisely in the air.

The best way to learn développé is calmly. Don't panic. Aim for

> absolute balance on the supporting leg
> absolute control of the working leg
> good turn-out in **both** legs
> creamy, continuous movement

Start practising développé by doing just one to the front, to the side, to the back, and to the side — and don't try to lift your leg too high when you open it from passé. After you've held it in the air a moment in each direction, lower it carefully to tendu and then slide your foot into 5th position. Count slowly, like this:

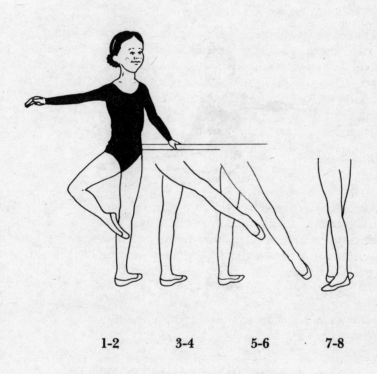

1-2          3-4          5-6          7-8

Remember to close your side développé in 5th position behind, so you'll be ready to développé back.

If you feel really strong and brave after you've done that on both legs, return to your original 5th position, right foot front, and repeat the entire exercise again. This time, see if you can développé straight out from your hip, so your working leg is parallel to the floor when it's fully extended.

Where do you feel the extra stretch? Probably in the big muscles on top of your thighs. If they do all the work, of course they'll hurt. Use the big ones under your thighs and in your bottom as well. They can push the leg up from underneath while the top muscles pull it up from above.

## Port de bras

When you learn the leg movements for these développés, you should learn the port de bras that goes with them. Although you usually hold your arm still when you're working at the barre, its movement is an important element in adagio. It gives you a longer, more graceful line, and it'll help you keep your balance too.

Your working arm passes through three separate positions during each développé, but you should move it from one to the next without a bump or a pause. That arm is held to the side when you begin your développés, just as it is in almost all the other exercises.

When your foot leaves the floor,

your arm curves down by your side.

As your foot travels up to
passé,

your arm swings gently up in
front of you.

As your leg extends in
développé,

your arm opens again to the
side.

It stays to the side as you lower
your leg and close your 5th
position.

Repeat this port de bras with each développé. It
should flow as smoothly from your shoulder as
your leg flows from your hip.

The movements of your legs, arms, and head can be combined in so many different ways that no one can count the number of adagios the human body can perform. You could make dozens of changes in this développé sequence.

Why don't we try just two, to give you an idea of the enormous variety of adagio movements.

## Fondu

First, let's add a *fondu* to it. Fondu is another of those movements that you already know without realising it. The word means sinking down. Can you guess what the movement would be? How could you lower your body in the middle of an adagio? Well, you can't sit down and remain standing on one leg at the same time, so the answer can't be sitting down. And I hope you won't *fall* down. What about simply bending the leg you're standing on? That's it exactly. **Fondu is a demi-plié on only one leg.**

Let's add the fondu to the first développé sequence, when your working leg isn't lifted very high. You'll need to add another four beats to your counting in order to fit the fondu in — two counts to plié on your supporting leg, and another two to straighten it again.

85

The entire, uninterrupted movement now goes like this:

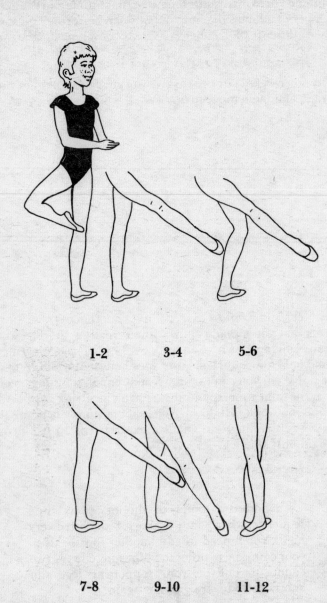

1-2      3-4      5-6

7-8      9-10      11-12

Do one développé in each direction like this, inserting the fondu after you've extended your working leg. But change nothing else! The positions of your arm and working leg, your strong turn-out, and your careful tendu and 5th position must stay just as they were before.

## Retiré

Want to try one more different adagio? This is a slightly shorter and quicker one. It exchanges the bend in your supporting leg — fondu — for a bend in your working leg. The new bend is called *retiré*.

In retiré, your legs look like this.

Does that position look familiar?
Isn't it exactly the shape your
legs form when you do a passé?

The difference between passé and retiré is not the shape, but the way you move to make that shape.

In **passé**, your working foot starts on the ground and moves into that position.

In **retiré**, your working foot is already in the air when it starts moving there.

So retiré is really a linking step for you to use between développés. It gives you a new choice: instead of lowering your leg to tendu and 5th position after each développé, retiré allows you to keep it in the air, folding and opening again and again, like the wings of a butterfly.

It takes real strength to move like a fragile butterfly. Your supporting leg will have to carry all your weight for as long as you sandwich retirés between développés. And your working leg won't get a rest on the floor until the end of the entire sequence.

Just to find out what it feels like, do four développés, one in each direction, with a retiré after each one. Tendu and close to 5th after the last développé. After the first passé and développé, your arm should remain to the side. Each movement should receive two full counts.

1-2          3-4          5-6

7-8          9-10

11-12          13-14

15-16

No lopsided practise allowed.

No tilting, leaning, or poking out tummy or bottom.

Whatever you do on one leg, you must do on the other leg.

Whatever you practise with one hand on the barre, you must practise with the other hand on the barre.

No teacher would ever ask you to do all four of those adagios one right after the other. You'd collapse.

Choose one of the sequences each time you practise

| low développé | high développé |
|---|---|
| développé with fondu | développé with retiré |

and concentrate on getting every moment of it just right. Don't be discouraged if you can't lift your leg very high or hold it very long at first. The strength and control you need to dance beautifully will develop gradually, as you continue to practise. Even the greatest dancers take class every single day of their lives, to improve their grace and control and build up their strength. They began right where you are now — so don't give up!

## Grands Battements

The last step you perform before you leave the barre is big, bold and energetic, a welcome change after the sustained effort of adagio. What you and I call high kicks, dancers call *grands battements*.

Keep both hips square to the front and your arm relaxed and curved to the side. Then, without bending your back or either knee or anything at all, **kick** as high as you can. Really let your leg go — let it fly right out of your hip socket. Hold your turn-out as always. Hold your proud, erect posture. And aim your foot right toward the ceiling. A rousing march is wonderful music for grands battements because its powerful beat and rhythm exactly match the movement.

Begin in 5th position and do four grands battements in each direction, putting the accent on the sharp, straight upswing of your leg.

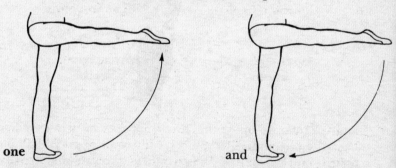

one                                        and

You'll have to tilt your body slightly forward to get a good kick behind you, but don't let yourself slump. And line your top half up over your hips and bottom half the moment you begin your last four battements to the side. Don't kick so high that you knock yourself over, but don't be stingy with your energy either.

## Balançoire

*Balançoire*, a variation of grand battement, is even more fun to do. There are no 5th positions in it, no kicks to the side, and for once, instead of holding your body still and upright, you're allowed to move it while you move your leg.

In balançoire, your working leg swings like the clapper of a bell, first in front of you and then behind, passing straight through 1st position in between. As it swings, your body should lean **away** from the direction it's moving.

When your leg swings forward,
your body tilts back.

When your leg swings back, your body tilts forward

That tilt will help you balance, and give you the longest stretch in your leg, back, and tummy muscles.

Begin balançoire with your working foot pointing back in tendu that will give you a headstart on your first forward battement. Then **swing** your leg, sixteen times in all, brushing through a clean 1st position after each battement and keeping that leg turned out the whole time.

Finish neatly in 1st position after you've counted sixteen — and I mean finish! Stop moving after 16 swings! You may be out of breath, red in the face or very tired, but should keep control of your body to the very end of each movement. That's what good dancing is all about.

# IN THE CENTRE

The work you've done at the barre has taught you many ballet steps and several ways to combine them. You've also learned to centre your body's weight and to maintain an erect, relaxed posture. The barre has guided you onto your balance, and even supported you at times, I'm sure. All this is your preparation for the same kind of dancing professionals do on stage in front of an audience. Do you feel ready to let go of the barre and start dancing on your own as they do? I hope so, because now's the time to do just that.

As you move out onto the floor, look around carefully. You're about to add two wonderful elements to your dancing, and you should think hard about their importance.

The first is **space**. You now have lots of room to dance in, and you must use it. Many young dancers are afraid to step out and move freely in all the space around them. Perhaps they think their mistakes will be more noticeable if they dance so boldly. Well, they're right. Any mistakes you make *will* be more noticeable if you're a big, brave dancer, and that's just what you want. If you can't see your mistakes, you can't correct them.

On the stage, a shy dancer is as vague and indistinct as a shadow and even less interesting to watch. And a timid student will never learn to *be* a dancer at all.

The space around you in the studio should be no more frightening than the playground or the garden, where you run and jump and play every day. Use as much space as you can, and enjoy it!

As for mistakes, the second new element in your dancing will help you solve those. There's no audience to make you nervous or shy in the classroom, but there is a **mirror** and now it's right in front of you. It will be watching you all the time, noting every move you make, just like the audience which will one day watch you dance.

Try to please the mirror as you would the audience, and pay attention to the dancing it shows you. A chance to see yourself dance is a chance to correct your dancing. Don't let that chance slip away.

# PLACEMENT AND BALANCE

Now, to be sure you *can* stand firmly on your own without the barre, you should begin your centre practice with short, simple exercises for balance and placement. If you've been dancing correctly at the barre, these won't give you any trouble. But if it's hard to do them without lots of wobbling, you've been cheating at the barre — cheating yourself — and everything that follows will be even harder.

For all these exercises, carry your arms in a wide 2nd position, sloping them gently from your shoulders so your hand floats in the air between your shoulder and waist.

Try a set of tendus with demi-plié first. From 1st position, do two smooth and easy ones in each direction. A waltz count of three should take the edge off any jerky or jagged movements.

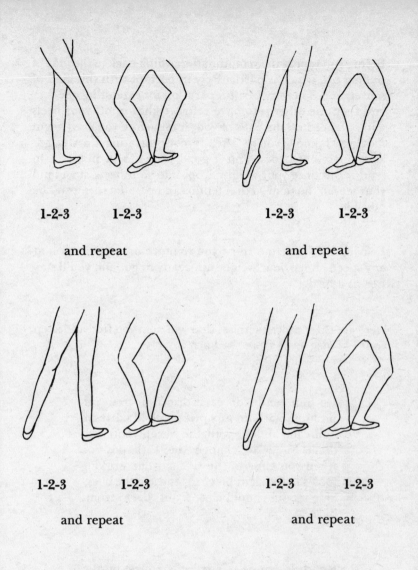

**1-2-3**          **1-2-3**                    **1-2-3**          **1-2-3**

and repeat                              and repeat

**1-2-3**          **1-2-3**                    **1-2-3**          **1-2-3**

and repeat                              and repeat

Then repeat the whole series with the other foot.

You could also do every tendu on alternate feet,
as if one foot were chasing the other out of 1st
position after each demi-plié.

Before you repeat that combination, think back to the idea of pulling up, which is particularly important with this kind of movement. The very best preparation for extending one foot and then the other is to have your weight up, off your heels and balanced on the balls of your feet, before you even begin moving. I know you're already concentrating on straight knees, stretched toes, and a good turn-out in plié *and* in tendu. But once your weight drops into your heels, it will pin your feet to the floor so that tendus and pointed toes won't be possible.

Leaving the barre has freed you to move in any direction at any speed. Keep your weight up, ready to go, and you'll stay free as a bird.

Here are three more exercises that will help you find and keep your balance away from the barre.

1. Do four **tendus** in each direction from 5th position, **without any plié** at all. Make them light and quick, with the accent out, and don't forget to change your 5th position when you close to the side so your working foot is in the right place to tendu to the back. Side tendus should close front, back, front, back.

2. **Rond de jambe par terre** is a little harder than tendu, because your working leg doesn't stop underneath you until it's travelled all the way around you. Do this sequence slowly so you don't get your directions mixed up.

From 1st position, do four ronds de jambe **en dehors** with your right foot, then four en dehors with your left. En dehors means outward; the working foot moves forward first and then around and out of sight.

Then do four ronds de jambe **en dedans** with your right foot, and another four en dedans with your left foot. En dedans means inward; your working foot reaches behind you first and then glides around into your line of vision.

Pass your foot through a perfect 1st position after each half-circle, and count three as you did at the barre — 1 for each straight movement and 2, 3 for each half-circle.

OR

3. Finally, try four tiny **dégagés** in each direction from 5th position. Change your 5th when you dégagé side, and don't forget to put your heel down after **every** dégagé. Your foot should brush the floor like a feather, whisking into the air without a sound and fitting back into 5th position without a jolt.

If you did **all** of these sequences every time you practised, you'd be exhausted. Any two will give your body plenty to do and your mind plenty to think about. Practise them with your full attention, and you'll be surprised how quickly your strength and confidence will grow.

# ADAGIO

It's natural to feel a little flustered after your first unsupported steps in the middle of the floor. And it's easy to forget about line and large, clear positions when you're fumbling with the details of small precise movements like dégagé and rond de jambe. That's why it's always a good idea to practise adagio next. Its slow tempo and stately shapes will calm you down and put the flowing line back in your dancing. Let me show you two new positions which are often the high points of an adagio.

## *Arabesque*

Does this look familiar?
It could be a grand battement
to the back, couldn't it?

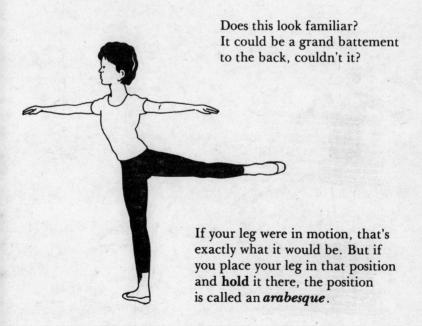

If your leg were in motion, that's exactly what it would be. But if you place your leg in that position and **hold** it there, the position is called an *arabesque*.

You can arrange your arms and head almost anywhere, and lift your leg very high or just a few inches off the floor. But any time that straight leg is held straight behind you, with your hips held square to the front, you're in arabesque.

## Attitude

If you hold a **bent** leg in the air — either to the front, the side, or the back of you — the position is called an *attitude*.

Your raised leg must always be turned out, and your knee must always be higher than your foot.

This position is nearly the same, but since the knee is dropping towards the ground, it's definitely **not** an attitude.

You've already passed through attitude positions when you were practising adagio at the barre. Can you find the attitudes there? Attitude is hidden in développé. Your working leg goes right by it each time it straightens from passé or folds up into retiré.

Since you didn't include either arabesque or attitude in your adagios at the barre, let's fit them in now. As you work on adagio, you'll slowly build the poise and muscular control to shape these two positions naturally and display them beautifully.

Adagio sequences are usually performed in eight-count phrases, just like many of your exercises at the barre.

You could start practising with a simple adagio like this one: from 1st position, to the front, side, back and side. Passé on counts 1 − 2, développé on 3 − 4, *hold* on 5 − 6, tendu on 7, close on 8.

That's identical to your développé sequence at the barre, only now you're clearly holding your working leg in arabesque.

Are you having trouble keeping your balance?

Well, is your:

Torso centred?

Shoulders even and relaxed?

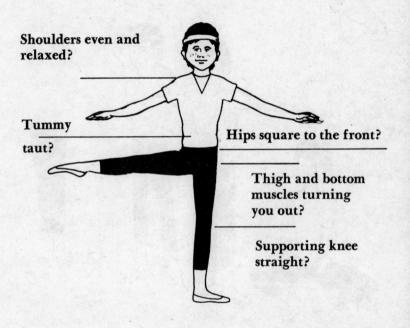

Tummy taut?

Hips square to the front?

Thigh and bottom muscles turning you out?

Supporting knee straight?

Weight pulled out of your heels?

Tension makes you strain and strain makes you wobble. Tension also jabs sharp corners and angles into your line where you least want them. Isn't this much nicer?

There are as many different adagios as there are different snowflakes, so you must learn to expect the unexpected. Begin the next adagio with a grand plié in 1st position

1-2-3-4          5-6-7-8          1-2-3-4          5-6-7-8

and follow that with a high relevé, lifting your arms over your head.

Then, to the front, side, back and side, do tendu, attitude front, retiré and close in to 1st.

1-2          3-4

5-6          7-8

Repeat the entire sequence, starting with the grand plié, with your left leg as the working leg. And remember to pull your knee way 'round to the side every time you retiré.

You could also change that adagio by adding a fondu. Try it that way: each time your working foot slides away from you in tendu, fondu — that is, demi-plié — on your supporting leg. That supporting leg pulls up straight again as the working leg leaves the ground and moves into attitude. It would look like this:

1-2                3-4

5-6                7-8

Here's another variation, with the demi-plié in a different place. Try this one from 5th position:

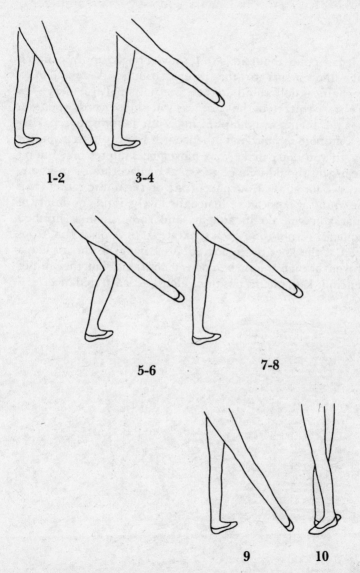

1-2      3-4

5-6      7-8

9      10

You can always return to the barre and practise any of these adagios there if you want to. Holding on again might give you an extra dose of confidence the next time you try them on your own.

One last point about adagio. It's not enough simply to match your movements to the proper counts. A robot or a mechanical doll would do that, but not a ballet dancer. Try to **phrase your steps** the same way you phrase words when you speak. Dancing without phrasing is just as boring as speaking in a monotone, and no audience will want to watch you for long if you don't make your movements interesting. I don't mean you should change the steps or decorate them in any way — not at all. But concentrate on the music rather than the counts. Show the audience the lovely, fluid continuity of what you can do in adagio, and show them a finished sequence rather than each separate step. A passé that stops dead at the knee or an attitude that hangs in the air like a broken branch might be correct positions, but they're not dancing. Don't learn positions alone — learn to dance.

# JUMPS

I know what you're thinking. You're thinking, 'All the dancers *I've* ever seen do more than stand in one place all the time. They run and jump and turn too.' Right you are! Did you think you'd never get that chance yourself? Well, here goes!

## Sauté, changement and soubresaut

After all the careful control of those adagios, I'll bet you're ready to explode with energy. Do it! Explode straight up into the air with sixteen big, bouncy jumps from 1st position. Carry your arms low and your head high, straighten your legs completely in the air, and point your toes hard. And don't forget the most important rule of jumping:

> **Each time you land, force your heels down into the floor and force your knees out in demi-plié.**

That will put the coiled spring in your legs that will shoot you into the air like a rocket.

Every jump in ballet is a *sauté*. Since there are bigger jumps to come, you might want to prepare for them by doing four very small, quick sautés — with your toes barely leaving the floor — in 1st, 2nd, 4th, and 5th position.

But here's a surprise. Once you're in 5th position, a sauté becomes two different jumps, each with its own name.

> If you leave the ground with your right foot in front and land with your right foot still in front, you're performing a *soubresaut*.

> If you leave the ground with your right foot front and land with your *left* foot in front, you're executing a ***changement***, one of the most common jumps in ballet. You've already changed 5th position on the ground — in tendu and dégagé — so doing it in the air, where you don't even have to support your own weight, shouldn't be a problem.

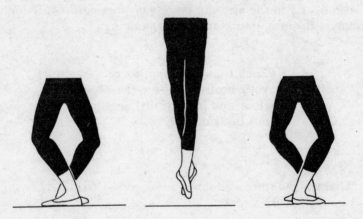

Try combining the two jumps in a single series. Start in 5th position with your right foot front and your arms held low. Do four soubresauts in place and then four changements in place. Follow those with four soubresauts travelling forward, and another four moving backward. The last four should return you to the spot where you started jumping. Which foot have you got in front now? It should still be the right one.

Soubresauts can carry your body in any direction at all, but you must always move in one piece,

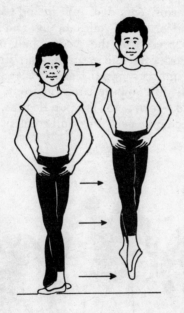

**never** feet first and body afterward.

Think of a piece of popcorn jumping around in a hot pan. It never leaves a part of itself behind to catch up later. Everything jumps at once — and so should you.

## Échappé sauté

Sauté, changement and soubresaut are all jumps from two feet to two feet. *Échappé* is another one. Remember practising it back at the barre, when you were first learning relevé? As a jump, it should properly be called *échappé sauté*.

Stand in 5th position, right foot front, arms low. Demi-plié for preparation. Then, as you jump straight up, flash your legs apart in the air and open your arms. Your demi-plié in 2nd position will take the jolt out of your landing, and it will also prepare you for the second half of the échappé. Push from 2nd position, jump straight up again, and scissor your legs together so you land in 5th with your **left** foot in front. Your arms should return to the low port de bras. Each complete échappé needs two full counts:

preparation     **and**     1

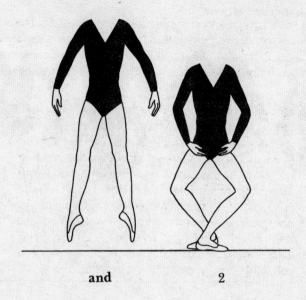

**and**                    2

Of course, the slower you count, the longer you'll have to stay in the air and the bigger your demi-plié and push will have to be.

Try doing four *giant* échappés, a total of eight very slow counts, changing your 5th position each time you bring your legs together.

See if you can keep your body over the same spot on the floor the whole time, without travelling forward, backward, or to either side.

Or, if you'd prefer a faster exercise, mix low échappés with tiny changements, like this.

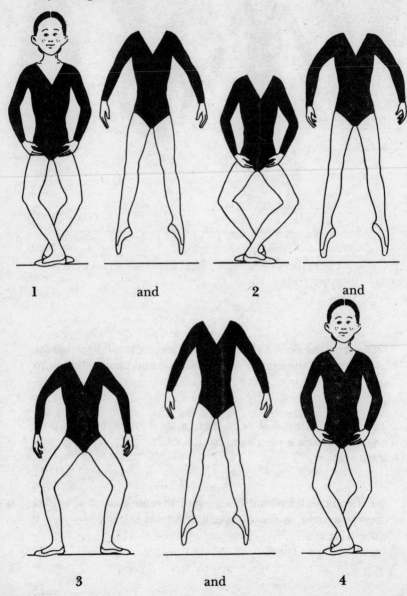

1      and      2      and

3      and      4

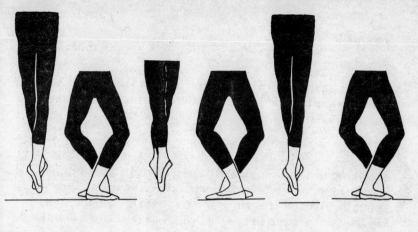

changement          changement          changement

5                   6                   **7**,
                                        hold count
                                        **8** and
                                        repeat.

Those steps should look like the rat-a-tat-tat of a
drum roll — short, sharp, and clear.

Want to rest a while and catch your breath? You certainly
deserve a break after all that jumping. But wait a minute!
**Don't sit down** whatever you do, or all your careful warming
up will go to waste. You can sit down or even lie down once the
class is over, but until then you must stay on your feet to keep
your muscles from going slack and limp.

If you're out of breath, clamp your mouth closed and breathe
through your nose. You'll get all the air you need, and your
breathing will gradually return to a normal rate. And if your
legs feel weak and woolly, stop dancing for a moment and
simply walk in a big circle around the room. Your muscles
and your mind will both relax, and after that little stroll,
you'll be refreshed and ready to dance again.

117

## Assemblé

I'll teach you one more jump for two feet and then you'll have five to choose from when you practise. Like many ballet steps, this one takes its name from the action it demands of you.

*Assemblé* means assembled or put together. In this jump, you leave the ground with your legs separated, and assemble them or put them together again as you return to the ground. Both legs help you get into the air, but each one does it in a slightly different way. The jump looks like this:

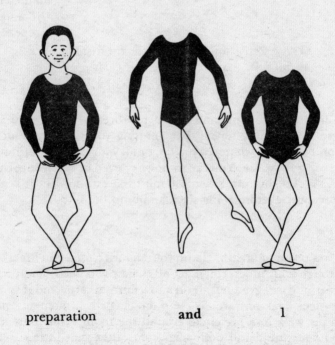

preparation                    **and**                    1

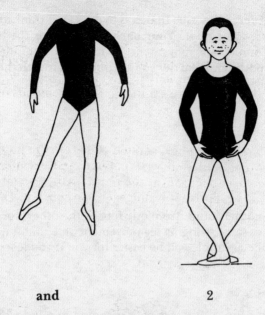

**and**                 2

What you're doing is this: After the demi-plié preparation,

> The **front** foot in 5th position pushes
> straight up and off the floor in sauté

> The **back** foot brushes out to the side
> and off the floor in dégagé

> Both feet leave the floor **at the same
> time** and return to it at the same time.

> And each time you jump, **the foot
> that began in back** and opened in
> dégagé, **closes in front.**

That's harder to describe than it is to do. Don't think about it too much — just do it. Your back leg performs the biggest and most important movement: as it goes to the side away from 5th position, it carries you **up** into the air with the force of its swing.

## *Jeté*

There's another jump, from one foot to the other, for which you use this same swinging leg movement and almost nothing else. Maybe assemblé will be easier for you if you learn to do *jeté* first.

Jeté means thrown — keep that meaning in mind while you practise the jump. Two things get thrown in jeté:

1. Your working leg is thrown in the air

2. Your body's weight is thrown from one leg to the other with every jump.

Start in 5th position, right foot back, arms low. You're going to push straight up off your left foot as your right foot brushes out to the side with a whoosh that helps lift you into the air. So far, jeté is exactly like assemblé. The difference is that in jeté you land on **one foot only**. Whichever foot has brushed out to the side — now your right foot — will whizz back into place under you, and all your weight will land on it. The other foot — in this case, the left — won't return to the floor at all. Instead, it will hide behind your right ankle, tucked up off the ground in sur le cou de pied.

Now, which leg do you think you'll throw out to the side for the next jeté? It has to be the left, doesn't it? That's the only one that's free to move since your right foot is holding you up. For your second jeté, the left foot brushes out to the side and up, and the right one pushes straight up from demi-plié. Throw your weight again and you'll land on the left, in demi-plié of course, with the right now hidden in cou de pied behind the left ankle.

preparation    **and**    1

**and**    2

121

Although your weight moves back and forth between one foot and the other, you don't actually move your body from side to side. Each jeté brings you right back to the spot you began on. That's another way that jeté and assemblé are the same. But remember:

**In assemblé, you land on two feet**

**In jeté, you land only on one**

And you must perform either one step or the other — there's nothing in between.

> If you've completely figured out the differences between the two steps, practise them separately. Starting with your right foot in back, do four assemblés — or eight if you feel strong — followed by four, or eight, jetés. The foot that swings up to the side will change each time you jump — right, then left, then right, then left, never the same foot twice in a row — but your body should stay in the same place right through to the last jump.

Can you make all the jumps the same height?

Can you make less noise than a cat?

If you can do all that, you're becoming a very fine ballet dancer indeed.

# TRAVELLING OR LINKING STEPS

Suppose you wanted to perform jeté or assemblé, or any ballet step, in different parts of the stage. You could walk from one spot to another, but you can dance over the distance too.

## Pas de bourrée couru

**Pas de bourrée couru** is an easy step to learn even though it has a long, difficult name. Pas means step, but bourrée has no translation — it's a name by itself, like Jenny or Steve. So pas de bourrée is a bourrée step, and couru means running, which tells you how to do it.

Actually, pas de bourrée couru isn't one step, but a whole string of them that run together like a string of pearls or the notes of a bird's song. Stand on demi-pointe in 5th position, arms low, right foot in front. Get **way up** on the tips of your toes — boys too! Then, staying on demi-pointe all the while, take a tiny step forward with your right foot and immediately move your left foot after it to close the gap in your 5th position. Do the same again: tiny step forward, close the gap. And again and again, faster and faster, until you really do seem to be running and your tiny steps shimmer across the floor.

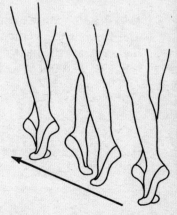

You can move forward or sideways to the right while your right foot is in front, and forward or sideways to the left while your left foot is in front.

But whichever foot starts in front stays there until another step comes along that lets you change your 5th position.

Here's a helpful practice sequence. Do four counts of pas de bourrée couru to the right, covering as much distance with as many little steps as you can in that time. On the count of 4, stop and lower yourself — without a thud — from relevé to demi-plié. Do little changements on counts 5, 6 and 7, and hold in demi-plié on count 8. Your left foot should be in 5th position front now, so you can go back the way you came.

Repeat again, once to the right and once to the left, and don't ever let your feet get too far apart. The minute the front one inches away, the back one should creep right up after it, like the head and tail of a caterpillar.

## Chassé

Pas de bourrée couru is a rather slow, gentle way to cross the stage. But every lively, energetic dancer like you needs to know a lively, energetic linking step as well as a small dainty one.

Instead of nibbling at space with your feet, you're going to learn to take great, big bites out of it with your legs. *Chassé* means chased; with one leg chasing the other across the floor and around the stage, you'll be travelling like the wind. Chassé can take you in any direction except sideways, and it works exactly the same way in every direction. **You always begin and end in 5th position demi-plié, and you always stretch one leg out and chase it with the other.**

Let's say your right foot is in front and you want to chassé forward.

1. Jump straight up to get yourself started. Raise your right arm over your head and curve the left one out to the side.

2. Put all your weight on your left leg as you land in demi-plié, and slide your right foot straight out in front of you in tendu. There's no weight on it, but your toes are still touching the floor.

125

3. Quickly tip your weight forward onto your right leg — which must bend at once — and stretch your left leg straight out behind you. Your toes should just touch the floor.

4. Now, as you jump straight up off your right leg, whip your left one up to meet it in mid-air. That's where the chase comes in: you slap your back leg against your front one to chase it forward. The moment you're in the air is the moment that one leg catches up with the other and chases it away.

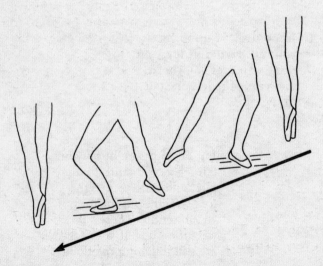

This fourth part of chassé, with both legs stretched straight beneath you, is really part 1 all over again. It ends the first chassé and starts the next one, all at the same time. Your right leg will slide forward again, and your weight will quickly shift from your back foot to your front one. Then the back leg will slap up against the front one and chase it ahead of you again.

I've broken chassé down into four parts for you, but it's actually performed in only two counts. The jump in the air is counted 'and,' while the skimming slide along the ground is 'one.'

Parts 2 and 3 of chassé happen so quickly and run into each other so smoothly that you can easily fit them into one count. I always think of the two parts as a single swinging movement. Your weight rocks from your back foot to your front foot as if you were sitting on a swing.

Practise chassé as if you were jumping from one swing to another, or — better yet — as if you were a monkey swinging from branch to branch in the jungle. You may not want to dance like a monkey, but you'll have fun trying to swing through the air and jump like one.

## Glissade

Chassé is perfect for covering long distances, but it's no good at all for travelling over short ones or connecting small jumps like jeté and assemblé. *Glissade* is the step you need for those short, neat journeys. The name means glide, and that's just what glissade is for. There's nothing big or flashy about it — it's just a very useful tool for travelling or for linking jumps.

Like chassé, glissade always begins and ends in demi-plié and in 5th position. But unlike chassé, either your front **or** back foot can move first in glissade. And you're allowed to change your 5th position while you're doing the step. Sometimes you begin and end with the same foot in 5th front. Other times, the foot that began the glissade in 5th front will end up in 5th back.

If you break glissade down into sections as we did with chassé, it looks like this:

That's what you actually do with each glissade, stretch each leg in turn as you move sideways. But it's easier to **think of glissade as an échappé**, like the one you did at the barre, **that carries you sideways**. A good dancer uses exactly the same scissor action of the legs for both échappé and glissade. Although you'll move through all those sections of the step every time you perform a glissade, it should feel and look like this:

| preparation | and | 1 | and | 2 |

And it **will** look like that too, once you've had a little practise.

Before you add any jumps to glissade, try the step all by itself. Start in 5th position, right foot back and arms held low and curved. Do three glissades to the right without changing your 5th position, and then one more **with** a change of 5th, so you finish the fourth glissade with your left foot back. Then do three glissades to the left, without changing, and a fourth with a change, so you finish with your right foot back again.

Don't sink down in your demi-plié; use it as a cushion for your heels and as a push for your next gliding movement. There are no bumps or jolts in glissade. And there won't be any off-balance wobbles either if you keep your body centred over your legs, whether they're in demi-plié or stretched to the side.

Another good reason to stay pulled up and centred is that you must always be ready:

**to change your 5th position**
**to jump in either direction**
**to move without very much warning or preparation.**

Ballet dancing demands all of that all the time.

Here's a glissade combination **with** jumps. Work it out slowly to begin with, but then try to perform it at a bright, even speed.

| Right foot back: | | |
|---|---|---|
| | Glissade right, don't change | and 1 |
| | Glissade right, don't change | and 2 |
| | Glissade right, don't change | and 3 |
| | Assemblé right — Right foot starts in back, closes front | and 4 |
| | Glissade left, don't change | and 5 |
| | Glissade left, don't change | and 6 |
| | Glissade left, don't change | and 7 |
| | Assemblé left — Left foot starts in back, closes front | and 8 |
| | Glissade right, change 5th | and 1 |
| | Glissade right, change 5th | and 2 |
| | Changement three times — left foot ends back | and 1,2,3. |
| | Glissade left, change 5th | and 1 |
| | Glissade left, change 5th | and 2 |
| | Changement three times — right foot ends back | and 1,2,3. |

Don't let your confusion upset you, and don't let it stop you either!

You can't learn to dance standing still. If you make a mistake or lose your way in the combination, stop for a moment, calm yourself down, and then pick up the steps again as soon as you can. That's hard to do when you're alone, but your classmates will continue dancing in the studio even when you stop. Watch them. Find your place in the sequence and try to complete it. You'll have lots of time to figure out your mistakes when the class is over. And you'll make fewer of them every time you dance if you don't let them get you down.

# TURNS

Now you've learned some jumps and some linking steps to connect them, but you still haven't done any turns. I'll tell you why. Ballet turns can be very tricky and very demanding. They require good balance, good muscular control and a strong sense of your position in space. You'll have to hold that position firmly in mind even when you can't see yourself, because if you turn completely around, you won't be able to watch yourself in the mirror the whole time you're turning.

The hard part of turning lies in guiding your body in two directions at once. You must keep it perfectly upright, head to toe, at the same time that you make it revolve around itself.

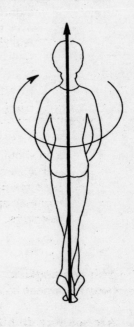

If you lose your plumb line and let yourself sag or flop, or slump your shoulders or bend your knees, you'll look like a corkscrew when you turn. And if you tilt your body sideways or forget to set your feet directly beneath you, you'll fall over like a top that's running down.

However, when you're *not* dancing, you turn all the time without any trouble at all. You turn in a game of tag or football, and the movement is just as natural to you as walking. Carry that ease and comfort into your ballet turns, and you won't have a moment's worry with them.

Some people lose their common sense when they first learn to turn. They don't want to look away from the mirror because they've made the mistake of locking eyes with their own reflection and believing that will hold them up. Don't make that ridiculous mistake yourself. Your muscles and your centred balance hold you up, no matter where you look.

Prove it to yourself before you develop any silly fears. Stand in 5th position, right foot front. Slowly raise both arms over your head and relevé so you're standing on demi-pointe. Then, using the bourrée you learned as a travelling step, turn in a complete circle.

You should look like a breathing statue, revolving on one spot with only the right foot moving and the left catching up to it in a steady stream of tiny steps.

This is a simple turn that gives you a chance to check your body from head to toe:

**Are you way up high on your relevé?**

**Is your weight pulled up and balanced equally on both legs?**

**Are your legs stretched, straight, and turned out from the hip?**

Is your tummy flat and your bottom pulled in?

Are your shoulders down even though your arms are up?

Did you fall over when you looked away from the mirror?

No, I thought not.

Practise this bourrée turn to the left as well; that is, start with your left foot front and turn in place to your own left. One direction might feel more comfortable, but turns are like every other movement in ballet — you must practise them to **both** sides without playing favourites between your right and left.

## Soutenu

A *soutenu* or sustained turn is also performed in one spot. But instead of inching yourself around with a series of little steps, you're going to pivot your entire body on the balls of your feet.

At first, each pivot will take you half-way around, but eventually you'll be able to make a complete turn without stopping.

Start in 5th position, left foot front and arms low. As preparation for the turn, slide your right foot to the side in tendu while you fondu on your supporting leg. Open your arms slightly to the side. Then, without bending your right knee, close the 5th position again by sliding your straight right leg in front of your left, and rise onto demi-pointe on both feet. Lower your arms beside you again.

That movement is really the beginning of the push that turns you around. All you have to do now is the pivot.

Stay in 5th position on demi-pointe, pulled up and turned out, and let your whole body continue around toward your left shoulder, as if the force of bringing your right foot in to 5th position was **pushing** you around.

Without your helping them in any way, your right heel and left heel will slip past each other as you pivot.

By the time you complete your pivot, you'll be facing the back of the room. You'll still be standing perfectly straight on demi-pointe, only your left foot will again be in front of your 5th position. Lower your heels. You've just done a soutenu turn.

Of course, you're now facing the wrong way, and you won't want to leave your back to the audience for long.

So, immediately repeat exactly what you've just done once. Slide your right foot out from 5th to tendu in 2nd, bring it back in front of 5th as you relevé, and let it push you around. Right heel will slip behind left as you turn and — presto! — there you are in your original position again, facing the front of the room.

It takes all those words to describe something that will happen quite naturally if you let it. A flick of the finger against your shoulder should almost be enough to whirl you up and around in soutenu. Practise soutenu to the right, with your left foot beginning in 5th position back and sliding out to tendu. And practise that sense of gossamer lightness too — let yourself turn like a weathervane in the wind. The more you relax, the better you'll dance and the more smoothly your turns will flow.

Experiment a little. See if you can complete an entire soutenu turn from a single preparation. The trick is to cross the working foot **over** the supporting one as you start to pivot. You may not be able to manage it quite yet, but give it a try. It's fun.

## Chaîné

It must seem to you that the only way to turn is to stay in one place. Not at all. One of the simplest turns in ballet can carry you so far — and so fast — that it's also used as a linking step. Its movements are repeated over and over again and linked together without a break, like the links of a chain. That's why it's called a *chaîné* turn.

If you want to cross any distance, you must take one step after another in the direction you want to go. That's exactly what you do when you walk — step follows step in a straight line. You don't even think about it. Chaîné turns combine progress along a straight line with the pivoting movement of soutenu. Each time you put your foot out on that line, you also make half a turn, using the same swinging push that flipped you around in soutenu.

Chaîné turns
look like this:

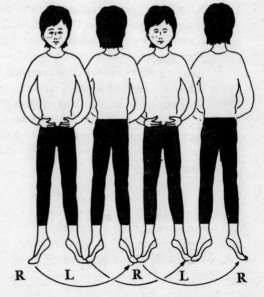

R  L  R  L  R

137

The compass you use for drawing circles in school is the perfect model for the linked movements of your legs.

**One foot anchors you to the ground
The other pushes you up and around**

Both legs stay completely straight while you turn, both heels stay up, and your weight shifts lightly from one foot to the other.

Stand all the way to the left
side of the room and point
your right leg and right arm in
front of you.

That's the preparation position for chaînés to the right. As you swing that foot from the front to the side, step up onto demi-pointe and look at the opposite wall to remind yourself where you're going. Then swing your left leg in a half-circle towards that wall, and immediately step up onto demi-pointe and shift your weight onto it. Then swing your right leg and arm around again, along the same straight line toward the other side of the room, and step up on your right foot.

Two rules to make you a whiz at chaîné turns:

1. Keep your legs quite close together. It's much easier to stay upright and continue moving in the right direction if you're not trying to take giant steps and balance your weight over the giant gap between your feet.

   When your legs stay close enough to whisper past each other, your chaînés will unwind like silk thread rolling off a spool.

2. ALWAYS look in the direction you're going!

That's impossible, of course. If you're going to turn your head and body in a complete circle, you can't watch the opposite wall **all** the time. But you can watch it *most* of the time if you learn to *spot*.

Here's how. Pick one spot on the wall you're moving towards and lock your eyes on it. It could be a clock, a picture or a window — it should be some sharply defined object that's easy to see. Now, forget your chaînés for a moment and simply turn yourself around very slowly, right where you're standing, keeping that spot in sight as long as you can. You'll have to keep your head still while your body starts to turn.

When you can't twist your neck any further, whip your head around in a flash. Your eyes will only leave your 'spot' for an instant, and they'll have it firmly fixed in view before your body has finished its slow turn.

If you spot while you chaîné, you won't wander all over the floor and you won't get dizzy. Your eyes will guide you along a straight path, and hold you erect at the same time.

It can take a long time to learn to turn and to learn to spot while you turn. Ballet dancers practise these steps every single day, and never stop trying to make them smooth and effort-less. Don't be annoyed with yourself if you find them puzzling at first — and don't stop trying. Your muscles have a memory all their own, and you have to help them memorise all these new movements by continuing to practise them.

# BIG JUMPS

As you approach the end of your ballet lesson, the boys may be asked to perform by themselves. For most of the class, boys and girls learn the same steps at the same time for the same reason — to develop strength, grace, and flexibility. But the daintiest steps and some turns, which women perform in stiffened pointe shoes, don't suit a man's body. And women's muscles are considered too small and light to lift them in some of the largest jumps.

## *Tour en L'air*

Here's one jump that only the boys have to practise. It's called a ***tour en l'air***, which simply means a turn in the air.

You know how to jump: demi-plié for preparation, then straighten your legs and point your toes as you rise into the air.

You know how to turn: push your whole body around as one unit, and spot to keep yourself from tipping or tilting.

Now put the two together. Begin in 5th with your right foot front and do two small changements in place to get yourself started. Make sure you land in solid demi-pliés, with both heels down on the floor, because you're going to need a big push for your tour en l'air.

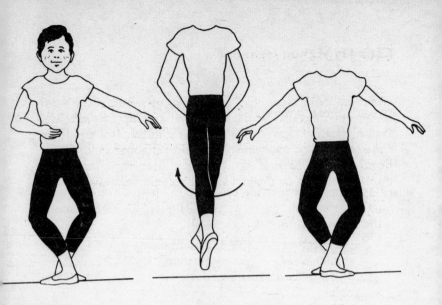

As you take off the
third time, turn
your entire body
around to the right.

Every part of you should turn at the same time — your
shoulders, chest, middle, straight knees and pointed toes
— and your feet should slip past each other in the air. When
you land, facing front exactly where you started, your left foot
should be in 5th position front.

Rest a minute to catch your breath, and then repeat the
combination to the left. Use a medium slow count of four: one
count apiece for each little changement, and two counts for
the tour en l'air. To help yourself get around, you can swing
your arms in the direction you want to turn as you start to
turn. But don't let them get ahead of you or they'll pull you off
balance. And don't count on them to turn you either. Let the
big muscles in your legs and stomach do most of the work —
that's what big muscles are for.

## *Changements en tournant*

Girls, you can practise tour en l'air with the boys if you want to, but you must stick to exactly the same counts they're using. If you prefer, you can share their music to try three *changements en tournant* — turning changements. If you begin the combination with your right foot front, you'll turn around yourself to the right. If your left foot starts front, you'll do

| | |
|---|---|
| changement — right foot to front | 1 |
| changement — left foot to front | 2 |
| 3 changements turning to left;<br>right,<br>    then left, then right closes front | 3, and, 4 |

as the boys do

| | |
|---|---|
| changement | 1 |
| changement | 2 |
| tour en l'air | 3, and, 4. |

It's easy to complete a full turn in three jumps, but it takes effort and concentration to make those changements small, bright, and sharp while you're turning.

## Grand jeté

With jumps like tour en l'air and changements en tournant, you shoot into the air like a firecracker, spiralling straight up from the ground and showering energy all around you.

*Grand jeté* is just the opposite — you perform it as if you were a comet, stretching your legs in space and flinging yourself forward in a long line with each jump. Grand jeté is a 'large, thrown' jump, larger than any jump you've learned yet. It's so big that you'll want lots of space to practise it. A large room is better than a small one, and grand jeté will be easier still if you're travelling along a diagonal path.

Start at the back left corner of the room with your left foot pointed in tendu toward the far right corner. Take two small steps — left foot, then right — to give yourself a running start, and then swing your left leg straight up in front of you in grand battement. Push off your right foot and **throw** yourself up and forward in jeté. Stretch both legs while you're in the air — that's what makes you look as if you're flying.

Keep your back leg stretched in the air as you land in demi-plié on your left foot, and then start the sequence again at once. Your right foot is free, so you'll run right, run left, grand jeté right. Then without a pause, do it all again: run left, run right, jeté left. The counts echo your movements:

| run | run | JETE |
|-----|-----|------|
| 1   | 2   | 3    |

Keep your running steps small and springy, and your grands jetés as long and stretched as you possibly can. You may only have room to do two or three of them on one diagonal, but that's fine. You can always go back to the corner and start again.

Always alternate corners when you practise anything on the diagonal. Your second series of grands jetés should start in the back right corner of the room with your right foot extended in tendu.

Your arms alternate too when you do grand jeté.

The right one reaches out and ahead of you when your left leg sweeps forward and up

The left one reaches forward when the right leg does the jeté.

Hold both rounded arms in front of
you in between jetés, and make them
swing forward as you jump — it will
help lift you into the air.

When you're stronger, you can leave out the running steps
and travel the whole length of the diagonal in grands jetés,
jumping on every count. But you'll find that the only way to
jump and jump and jump, without stopping or adding small
steps, is to use your demi-plié as if it were a trampoline. You
won't be able to push **off** the floor with every step unless you
push down **into** it every time you land.

# CLOSING MOVEMENTS

The last exercises in a ballet class are usually *grands battements* and *port de bras*, slow fluid movements that give you a chance to erase the tension from your body and return to a balanced, centred posture. Many students tie themselves in knots trying to turn and jump. And even professional dancers need some quiet steps at the end of a class to relax their minds and muscles before they leave the studio.

Grands battements to the side will stretch the lower half of your body — feet, calves, thighs, bottom and tummy. Start in 5th position, right foot back, arms held open to the side, and do four grands battements moving forward. That is, lift your back leg and close it in 5th position front each time you battement.

Then do another four moving back; front foot lifts and then closes behind. Let your foot carry your leg into the air each time, and try to float your weight up out of your heels as you were doing at the start of class.

A strong, thumping march is the ideal music for grands battements, as long as you resist thumping your working leg closed in 5th position.

Your accent should be up and out. Even if you're tired, you must control every movement of your body until you leave the studio.

Put your feet in 1st position, stay well pulled up and turned out, and a final port de bras will stretch and relax your middle, shoulders, arms and neck. Give yourself four very slow counts to reach each new position, and four more to return to a balanced, upright one.

# BOWS

What happens at the end of a ballet performance? The audience claps and the dancers bow to thank them for their attention and applause. Like everything else a dancer does on stage, the bows are learned in the studio and practised time and time again.

The ballet name for a man's bow or a woman's curtsey is *révérence*. At the end of class, your révérence is usually directed towards your teacher, as a mark of respect and a gesture of thanks. The movements themselves are very simple.

Boys, just put your feet next to each other, let your arms hang naturally at your sides, and bow your head.

Girls, your révérence is in two parts.

1. Tendu from 1st position to the side, opening your arms slightly

2. Cross your extended foot behind your supporting leg, and bend both knees in demi-plié as you bow your head.

You can easily repeat this small gracious bow to the other side. Step out to the side on whichever foot is now free, and cross the other behind it. Bend both knees, bow your head, and you've made your second curtsey.

Your class is over. If you've tried most of the steps I've shown you, and begun to master them, you're well on your way to being a ballet dancer.

# FAMOUS DANCERS

During the early history of ballet, several great dancers changed the art in ways which have survived right to the present. You should know a little bit about those dancers.

## Marie Camargo

Two hundred and fifty years ago, a lively dancer named Marie Camargo shocked audiences in Paris in two important ways. First she raised her long skirts several inches off the floor when she danced to show off her twinkling feet. And then she beat her feet and ankles together when she jumped, as only male dancers had done until then. She was the first woman to do both things, and she changed the history of ballet forever by doing them.

## Marie Taglioni

One hundred years later, in 1832, Marie Taglioni wore the first long, gauzy tutu in *La Sylphide*, a Romantic ballet written for her by her father. Taglioni looked especially like a spirit because she danced in pointe shoes.

Slippers with thick, stiffened toes had been introduced around 1800, when the stiffness in them came from darning the toes with heavy thread. At that time too, wires helped women balance on their tiptoes. But strong shoes with greater support became more and more common, and Taglioni's fairy-like appearance in them made them essential for women ever after.

Camargo and Taglioni danced hundreds of years ago, but the stars of Serge Diaghilev's Russian ballet company lived and performed at the beginning of this century. Anna Pavlova, Tamara Karsavina, and Vaslav Nijinsky are three of the greatest names in the history of ballet.

## Anna Pavlova

Anna Pavlova spent the first half of her life in Russia. She danced the leading roles in such great ballets as *Giselle*, *Swan Lake* and *The Sleeping Beauty*, and reached the rank of prima ballerina by the age of 25.

Between 1907 and her death in 1931, she travelled to corners of the world that had never seen ballet before, bringing it to South and Central America, Japan, China, Africa and Australia. Ivy House, her London home, is now a museum to her life and work. Those who saw her grace and artistry in performance, particularly in solos like *The Dying Swan*, called her a genius of dancing.

# Vaslav Nijinsky

Vaslav Nijinsky had the shortest, saddest and most spectacular career of any famous male dancer. He was already a leading dancer (*premier danseur*) at the age of nineteen when he joined Diaghilev's company. In the next 5 years, he created roles in twelve new ballets, two of which he choreographed himself, and danced the leading roles in the older works as well.

He was a wonderful actor with
a dazzling classical technique
of beats, turns and high leaps.
It was said that he could cross
and entire stage in only two
grands jetés. Tragically,
Nijinksy went mad before he
reached the age of thirty, and
never danced again.

# Tamara Karsavina

Tamara Karsavina was Diaghilev's female star and a frequent partner of Nijinsky. Her creation of the leading roles in Michel Fokine's ballets — *Les Sylphides, Carnaval, Petrouchka, Le Spectre de la Rose* and *Firebird* — and in Leonide Massine's more realistic ones revealed her genius for totally transforming her body and personality to suit each character. After retiring, she returned to the stage briefly to dance with Ballet Rambert in London. She also honoured the dancers of the Royal Ballet with her coaching and advice. She died in London in 1978.

# Alicia Markova

Alicia Markova began her long, international career when she joined Diaghilev's Ballets Russes at the age of fourteen. After his death, she danced in London with Ballet Rambert during its first years, and created several lovely roles in Ashton's early ballets. She then joined the very young Royal Ballet (then the Vic-Wells Ballet) where, as the company's first prima ballerina, she was the first British dancer to dance the leading roles in *Giselle* and *Swan Lake*. In 1950, she and Anton Dolin founded the Festival Ballet. Markova was a dancer of great lightness and delicacy. She passes on the exquisite details of her art today by lecturing and teaching.

# Anton Dolin

Her partner Anton Dolin began his career as a child actor. He danced with Diaghilev's company for five years — creating some roles, taking over others, and partnering all the company's stars — and then performed in England and around the world. His strength, like Markova's, lay in his classical technique and manner, and he was one of the great partners of this century, with a special gift for presenting and assisting the woman with whom he was dancing. He was the first English male dancer to win international fame, and he is internationally known as well for his productions of the classic ballets. He has written and lectured about his art and his career, and still coaches young dancers in the refined, classical style.

# Rudolf Nureyev

Rudolf Nureyev studied folk dancing as a little boy in Russia, but he didn't attend formal ballet classes regularly until he was seventeen. That is a very late age to begin training for a ballet career, and his teachers at the famed Kirov School in Leningrad thought he would be either a great dancer or a complete failure. He graduated from the school into the Kirov Ballet and immediately danced the leading roles in most of the nineteenth-century classics and several modern ballets. But he decided to leave this company, and to leave Russia, when he was twenty-three years old. A year later he made his Covent Garden début, partnering Margot Fonteyn in *Giselle*, and became a permanent guest artist of that company and her partner as well.

Nureyev has danced brilliantly in classical and modern ballets, jazzy ones, modern works by the choreographers Martha Graham and Paul Taylor — he can even tap dance. His limitless technical gifts and riveting stage personality attracted a new audience for ballet, larger than ever before, that has continued to grow steadily.

His dancing has carried him around the world, and into films and television. He has been the best-known male dancer in the world for twenty years, and today is still one of the greatest dancers alive.

# Mikhail Baryshnikov

The career of another Russian dancer, Mikhail Baryshnikov, follows Nureyev's closely. Baryshnikov also trained at the Kirov school, danced in the Kirov company, and decided to leave Russia — he chose to perform primarily in America.

> His breathtaking high leaps and many effortless turns, matched with the elegant manner of a classical danseur, won him gold medals in two international ballet competitions. He received one medal at Varna in 1966 and the other in Moscow in 1969. He joined American Ballet Theatre shortly after defecting from Russia in 1974, and stepped into the leading roles in classical ballets like *Giselle* and *Swan Lake* and into new works like Twyla Tharp's *Push Comes to Shove*. He is now the company's artistic director, and has staged his own versions of the Petipa masterpieces, *The Nutcracker* and *La Bayadère*.

# Natalia Makarova

Natalia Makarova is the third famous Russian dancer who left the Kirov Ballet to dance in the West. The winner of the gold medal at the Varna competition in 1965, she is a fragile, delicate dancer with exceptional technical and dramatic gifts. Her moving performance of the title role of *Giselle* has been called one of the greatest of our time. She also dances *Swan Lake, The Sleeping Beauty, La Sylphide*, and modern ballets by Kenneth MacMillan and Antony Tudor, bringing emotional conviction and physical purity of movement to all of them. She is a ballerina at American Ballet Theatre, and has also danced as a guest artist with the Royal Ballet and around the world.

# Margot Fonteyn

Margot Fonteyn was one of the little swans in the corps de ballet when Alicia Markova was dancing the difficult leading role in *Swan Lake* for the Vic-Wells Ballet. Fonteyn began her ballet training in Shanghai, but completed it in England. Her growth as an artist and the development of the Royal Ballet, where she was eventually prima ballerina, marched along hand in hand.

She was one of the finest ballerinas of this century, displaying technique, line, musicality, and a gracious, engaging personality that, all together, became known as the English style of dancing. She was Frederick Ashton's principal inspiration, and created the leading role in dozens of his ballets over the years. For the last fifteen years of her long career, she was partnered by Rudolf Nureyev. Her mature serenity as a dancer and his youthful energy made their partnership particularly memorable.

## Antoinette Sibley

Antoinette Sibley is the first British ballerina to have received her entire formal training at the Royal Ballet's own school. In 1959, she danced Swanilda, the leading role in *Coppélia*, at the first Royal Ballet School matinée ever presented at the Royal Opera House, Covent Garden. Very shortly afterwards, she took on the challenging dual role of Odette-Odile in *Swan Lake* on extremely short notice. Her triumph in that role was the first of many triumphs. In *The Sleeping Beauty, The Nutcracker, Giselle, Cinderella,* and *Romeo and Juliet*, she proved herself the natural successor to Fonteyn and a distinguished classical ballerina in her own right. Ashton captured all the joyous sparkle and serene elegance of her dancing when he choreographed *The Dream* for her in 1964. She and Anthony Dowell began their celebrated partnership in that ballet. They were ideally suited to each other — both physically and temperamentally — and they danced splendidly together for many years.

## Anthony Dowell

On his own, Anthony Dowell offers the finest example of male classical dancing at the Royal Ballet. You could use his crystal-clear technique and pure line as the basis for a textbook about ballet dancing. The respected title of *premier danseur noble*, or leading noble dancer, fits him perfectly, whether he is dancing the princely roles in *Swan Lake* and *Giselle* or the roles he has created in Ashton's *The Dream* and Kenneth MacMillan's dramatic *Manon*. Dowell has appeared frequently with American Ballet Theatre in America and has partnered the great ballerinas of that company and of the Royal Ballet with both charm and dignity.

159

# USEFUL ADDRESSES

Royal Academy of Dancing
48 Vicarage Crescent
London SW11

Cecchetti Society
70 Gloucester Place
London W1

Royal Ballet School (lower)
White Lodge
Richmond Park
Richmond

Ballet Rambert
94 Chiswick High Road
London W4

Royal Ballet School (upper)
155 Talgarth Road
London W14

Imperial Society of Teachers of Dancing
70 Gloucester Place
London W1

International Dance Teachers Association
76 Bennett Road
Brighton,
Sussex,
BN2 5SL

## Monthly Publications

The Dancing Times
45 Clerkenwell Green
London EC1

Dance and Dancers
2 Old Pye Street
London SW1